JESUS

....

an eyewitness account

JESUS

an eyewitness account

Bill Myers

VICTOR BOOKS®

A DIVISION OF SCRIPTURE PRESS PUBLICATIONS INC.
USA CANADA ENGLAND

. . . .

Jesus: An Eyewitness Account is a study of the Book of John for high school students. It shows how to grow in friendship with Jesus Christ while growing in understanding of who He really is. Student activity booklets (Rip-Off Sheets) and a leader's guide with visual aids (SonPower Multiuse Transparency Masters) are available from your local Christian bookstore or from the publisher.

Unless otherwise indicated, Scripture is taken from the *Holy Bible, New International Version,* © 1973, 1978, 1984, International Bible Society. Used by permission of Zondervan Bible Publishers. Scripture references marked NASB are from *New American Standard Bible,* © the Lockman Foundation 1960, 1962, 1963, 1968, 1971, 1972, 1973, 1975, 1977.

Interior illustrations: John McPherson

Library of Congress Catalog Card Number: 88-60208
ISBN: 0-89693-606-6

Recommended Dewey Decimal Classification: 248.83
Suggested Subject Heading: YOUTH—RELIGIOUS LIFE

CONTENTS

· ·

. . . .
For Heinz Fussle . . .
a mighty man of God

A COUPLE OF NOTES BEFORE WE START

God's Word is the most powerful weapon in the universe—"sharper than any double-edged sword" (Hebrews 4:12). In fact when Jesus was battling it out with Satan in the wilderness it was the only weapon He chose to fight him off with.

What makes God's Word—the Bible—so powerful is that it's "God-breathed" (2 Timothy 3:16). Think about that a minute—God breathing His very life into the words of Scripture. Something with that authority has to be life-changing. And it is. The Bible says that God's Word:

- cleans us up (Ephesians 5:26),
- shows us what we're really like (James 1:23-25),
- encourages us (Romans 15:4),
- equips us to do good (2 Timothy 3:17),
- leads us to faith (Romans 10:17),
- shows us the way to be saved (James 1:21).

Pretty powerful stuff. To get the most out of it, here's what to do:

First: Read the portion of Scripture listed at the beginning of a section. Take your time—try to read just one section per sitting.

Second: Stop a moment and think about what God may be telling you.

Third: After you've waited on God, go ahead and read the commentary in this book.

Some people think they'll save time by plowing through and just reading this commentary. But they're only fooling themselves. God's words do the changing, not mine. Mine are only to help explain and get you to think. His are to radically change and transform your life.

CHAPTER ONE
FROM THE TOP

JOHN 1

HOWIE REVEALS THE SECRET
INGREDIENT OF HIS
JOHN THE BAPTIST CASSEROLE.

GOD JOINS THE HUMAN RACE
. . . .
Read JOHN 1:1-18

If anyone knew Jesus, John did. Not only was he a member of the Big Twelve, but he was also one of Jesus' closest friends. In fact he was one of only three people with Jesus when God the Father dropped by for a little social call (Luke 9). John was the only one Jesus asked to look after His mother when He was dying on the cross. And he was the only person Jesus appeared to when He described the end times in the Book of Revelation.

Talk about connected. I mean, if anybody knew Jesus, this guy did. So it's no big surprise that his account of Jesus' life is one of the most popular books in the Bible. For anyone even vaguely interested in getting to know Jesus better, this particular Gospel is definitely worth the read.

To kick things off, John wastes no time. He gets right to the point and begins by calling Jesus God:

> In the beginning was the Word, and the Word was with God, and the Word *was God.*
>
> > (verse 1, italics added)

Talk about gutsy. I mean, John's either trying to pull off one of the biggest con jobs in history—or he's stating an amazing fact. And if it's the latter, then there had better be plenty of other Scriptures to back it up.

Luckily for John (and us) there are:

> For by Him [Jesus] all things were created: things in heaven and on earth, visible and invisible,

whether thrones or powers or rulers or authorities; all things were created by Him and for Him.
(Colossians 1:16)

Christ Jesus . . . being in very nature God, did not consider equality with God something to be grasped, but made Himself nothing, taking the very nature of a servant, being made in human likeness.

(Philippians 2:5-7)

For in Christ *all* the fullness of the Deity lives in bodily form."
(Colossians 2:9, italics added)

Then of course Jesus Himself had a few words to say on the subject:

Anyone who has seen Me has seen the Father.
(John 14:9)

Father, glorify Me in Your presence with the glory I had with You before the world began.
(John 17:5)

I and the Father are one.
(John 10:30)

Jesus was not some "good teacher" like Buddha or Mohammed or those other guys claimed to be. According to John, the Bible, and Jesus Himself, He was something very different. According to them, He was *not* a good teacher. According to them, He was and is God.

Big difference.

And quite a claim. Let's see if they can back it up.

JOHN THE BAPTIST

Read JOHN 1:19-28

Picture it . . .

Some guy out in the roasting desert, wearing camel-hair clothing, eating locusts and wild honey, and telling people they'd better get their acts together because God's on His way.

Let's face it, if this fellow were around today we'd find a nice padded room with no sharp corners for him to call home. But there was something about the Baptist that people were taking seriously. He struck a universal chord—one that still rings true today. He hit upon that intangible feeling of guilt, the feeling that somehow, someway we've failed. And more important, that somehow, someway we need to wash ourselves from these failures, to be clean from these . . . "sins."

John finally got to be drawing such a crowd that the religious hotshots figured they'd better pay a little visit to check him out.

Now remember, at this time everyone and his brother were waiting for the Christ to appear. The Messiah, the Saviour of Israel, had been promised by God for thousands of years, and everyone was expecting Him to make His debut any minute. So it's little wonder that the first question out of the authorities' mouths is, "Are you the Christ?"

The Baptist's answer couldn't be clearer: "No way."

Next they ask if he is Elijah—the Old Testament prophet who was whisked up to heaven hundreds of years ago and who many thought would come back to announce the Christ.

Again John says no.

Next, they ask if he's the Prophet—somebody a lot of folks also thought would be showing up.

Wrong again.

In desperation, they chuck the true-or-false quiz and ask John point-blank, "Who are you?"

He answers by quoting from Isaiah, an Old Testament prophet who spent a lot of time writing about the coming Messiah:

> I am the voice of one calling in the desert, "Make straight the way for the Lord."
>
> (John 1:23)

In other words, "It's my job to tell you, 'Straighten out your lives, God's on His way!'"

By now the bigwigs are getting a little hot under the collar. They came to grill John, not to be preached at. So they demand to know, "If you're just a nobody, then who do you think you are, baptizing?"

John gives them an answer, but not one they're expecting. He says that standing right there among them is somebody they don't know—somebody whose sandals he's not even fit to untie.

For what it's worth, John's not talking about being a shoe salesman here. Untying sandals was considered such a low-level job that only slaves were supposed to do it. So John makes it pretty clear that he's not out there on some ego trip. Instead, he's there to prepare the people for somebody else—somebody he's not even fit to be a slave to.

Needless to say, he's got everyone's attention.

THE LAMB OF GOD
Read JOHN 1:29-34

What a strange description. If I saw God standing in the crowd, I'd probably come up with a little classier introduction than, "Behold, the Lamb of God." How about, "Behold, the Creator of the Universe!" Or, "Look! It's Him, it's God, the One and Only. Drop to your knees, folks; it's Supreme Ruler time!"

But not John. Instead, under the inspiration of the Holy Spirit, he introduces Jesus simply as "the Lamb of God, who takes away the sin of the world."

Why? If he's going to compare God to an animal, why not "Behold, the Roaring Lion," or the "Soaring Eagle"? Why some ninth-rate animal like a baby sheep?

First of all, it was the lamb that was used in the temple sacrifice. Every day one was killed in the morning and another in the evening to pay for the people's sins.

This sounds pretty cruel, but keep in mind that sin is pretty cruel. In fact it's deadly—and somebody has to pay for it. And, as unfair as it seems, I suppose it's better that an animal pay with its life than a human with his.

So in one sense John is saying, "Look, this is the lamb that God has supplied—this is the one who will suffer and die in our place for all our sins."

Another reason the analogy works is that the blood from a lamb is what saved the people of Israel just before the Exodus, when they were getting ready to leave Egypt.

Remember, despite all the miracles God was performing through Moses, Pharaoh would not let the

Israelites leave. So finally, to get His point across, God made plans to wipe out all of the firstborn in the country.

The only problem was the Israelites had a few firstborn too. How could they be protected while God carried out His judgment on the Egyptians?

The solution was simple. To be saved, the Israelites were to kill a lamb and smear its blood over their doors. Later that night, when the Angel of Death went from house to house to kill the firstborn, he'd see the blood over the Israelites' doorways and literally *pass over* the homes that were covered by the blood.

Again, some pretty interesting symbolism when you stop to think that it's Jesus' blood that saves us from eternal death.

There was one more ceremony that involved a lamb. The High Priest would lay his hands on a lamb (or goat) and transfer all of the people's sins onto the animal. The animal would then be taken as far away from the people as possible, way out in the wilderness, and let go.

So when John uses the phrase "Lamb of God," he is definitely making a statement. In essence he is saying, "Look, here's someone that will take all of your sins—every failure, everything you've ever done wrong—and dispose of them forever. He will take all that guilt, all that blame upon Himself. He will take the punishment that should be yours so you can be clean, so you can be free."

It's still that way today. Jesus will still take away our sins. We can still be clean; we can still be free; we can still live forever.

A pretty incredible deal when you stop to think about it—and ours just for the asking.

But . . . we do have to ask.

COME AND SEE
. . . .
Read JOHN 1:35-51

As soon as the Baptist introduced Jesus, people began to follow. In fact, Jesus' first two disciples were
originally the Baptist's disciples. Then, the next day
or so, Peter, Philip, and Nathanael also signed up.

Isn't it interesting that not one of these men was
convinced to follow Jesus by any great philosophical
debate or argument? Instead it was the simple decla-
ration of who Jesus is (by the Baptist) or the gentle
encouragement (once by Jesus and once by Philip)
to "come and see."

The same is true today.

You can't argue anybody into accepting Jesus as
Saviour. No amount of mental gymnastics or verbal
overkill will do the trick. It has to be something God
shows them; it has to be something they decide on
their own.

If you're reading this and don't know if you're
ready for all this Jesus stuff, don't expect me to convince you. Don't expect your friends or relatives to
convince you. That's between you and God. Check
Him out for yourself. "Come and see." Ask *Him* to
show you if He's real.

And you know something? If you're serious, He
will. It may not be overnight. But if you start reading
His Word and asking Him to reveal Himself, He will.

On the other hand, if you're already a believer and
want to see your friends and relatives saved, don't
cram it down their throats. Look for opportunities to
share your faith, yes, but don't try to con or fast-talk
them into the kingdom. You're not selling used cars
here; you're offering people friendship with God.

16

And friendship is not something you can argue anyone into.

I did not argue my wife into loving me. She did not argue me into marrying her. Our love and commitment to each other came as a result of knowing and trusting each other. The same is true about our relationships with God.

When Nathanael tried to pull Philip into a debate, when he hit him with, "Nazareth! Can anything good come from there?" Philip's only response was, "Come and see." The same should be true for us. When we talk to friends and loved ones, let's encourage them to get to know God, to read His Word. Ask them to look at what He's done in our lives. Explain what "the Lamb of God" did for us on the cross. *AND PRAY FOR THEM.* But let's not turn our witnessing into a philosophical argument.

Debates and fast-talking are for politicians and con artists—not lovers.

And what God wants is . . . our love.

CHAPTER TWO

. . . .

NO MORE RELIGION

JOHN 2–3

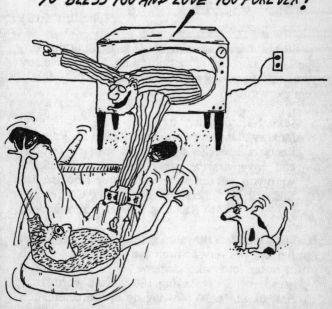

THAT'S RIGHT, SON! IF YOU DONATE
$500 TO OUR GOLD-PLATED CHOIR
LOFT FUND DRIVE, GOD HAS PROMISED
TO BLESS YOU AND LOVE YOU FOREVER!

YET ANOTHER REASON WHY SOME
CHRISTIANS SHOULDN'T OWN TVS.

WHY WINE?

Read JOHN 2:1-11

Now before anyone uses this section as an excuse to grab a six-pack and put down a few cold ones, let's get the whole picture. For starters, Scripture makes it pretty clear that boozing and believing don't mix.

> Do not get drunk.
>
> (Ephesians 5:18)

Over and over again the Bible talks about the dangers and stupidity of getting drunk. If you have any doubts, take a look at the company God puts drunkenness with:

> sexual immorality, impurity and debauchery; idolatry and witchcraft; hatred, discord, jealousy, fits of rage, selfish ambition, dissensions, factions and envy; *drunkenness,* orgies, and the like. I warn you, as I did before, that those who live like this will not inherit the kingdom of God.
>
> (Galatians 5:19-21, italics added)

But if God's so down on getting drunk, why, of all things, for His very first miracle did Jesus choose to turn water into wine? And we're not talking a few glasses here. We're talking 180 gallons worth!

First of all, Jesus' showing up at the celebration makes it pretty clear that He's not a pious killjoy: *Excuse me, are you having fun? Well, I'm sorry— you'll have to find another religion.*

But it doesn't make Him a party animal either.

What it *does* show is that He is perfectly comfortable celebrating and rejoicing with others at a wedding feast. The idea that He is some scowling, Bible-thumping, down-with-good-times fanatic just doesn't fit into the picture Scripture paints.

Secondly, running out of food or refreshment at a celebration of this importance would be pretty embarrassing. For months the newlyweds would be the joke of the town. Not exactly the way to start off a new life.

So Jesus, in His sympathy and understanding, chooses to take care of the little problem. (It's nice to know that even the little embarrassments of our lives are important to Him.)

But there's a third reason. The water in those stone pots was used to wash the people's hands and feet as part of a Jewish religious ceremony—a routine that was anything but interesting.

So by changing that water into wine, Jesus was making another clear statement. In essence He was saying, "I'm taking this dead, boring religion of yours and transforming it into something that is sparkling, something that is exciting and full of life!"

That's what Christ came to do. He came to do away with "religion." That's right. He came to destroy meaningless ritual and replace it with a dynamic, on-fire relationship—a relationship with God Himself.

Christianity does not have to be a cure for insomnia. Jesus said, "I have come that they may have life, and have it *to the full*" (John 10:10). He did *not* say, "I've come to bore you out of your skull."

But the choice is ours. We can keep Christianity just a religion. We can keep it boring and dull by playing it safe, by going through the ceremonial motions and traditions of *Churchianity* . . . or we can really begin pursuing Jesus and drinking His new

21

wine. We can really begin taking Him up on His promises. We can begin stepping out and putting His Word to the test in *all* areas of our lives. In short, we can begin living on that water-walking, cutting edge of His power.

And once that's happened—once we've tasted that new wine—I guarantee you, life will never be the same.

A LITTLE HOUSECLEANING

Read JOHN 2:12-25

There's a lot to think about in this section, but let's look at three major points.

First of all, John shoots down the theory that God is some kindly old duffer shuffling around heaven passing out hugs and kisses.

Now it's true "God *is* love." But for those who want to rebel, or worse yet, who want to rip off His kids . . . well, let's just say He's got another plan.

That's what we see in this passage. People would travel hundreds of miles to Jerusalem to worship God, only to discover their money was "not good enough" to give Him—or their animals were "not good enough" to sacrifice.

But, hey, no sweat. Lucky for them there just happened to be dozens of people inside the temple court who would gladly exchange their "dirty" money for "clean" money or sell them "acceptable" animals for sacrifice. The only problem was that these merchants would make up to 1,800 percent profit in the process!

No wonder Jesus was steamed. And we'd better believe His feelings haven't changed. For those who want to follow Him and who want to help their fellow human beings—there's love and understanding. For those who exploit and step all over people—there's still the whip.

JESUS' PROOF

After the little housecleaning, people begin grilling Jesus about who He thinks He is. I mean, pulling off a stunt like that calls for some pretty high authority. If He's claiming to be the Christ, He'd better get on the stick and make His point by impressing everyone with a few miracles.

But God will never be bullied, He'll never be manipulated. His miracles are used to love, to heal, to encourage—they are never to entertain or wow the curious.

So instead of putting on a sideshow, Jesus prophesies about His upcoming resurrection. But—as is usually the case with deep, spiritual truth—the people miss the boat. They think He's talking about an immediate, literal interpretation:

"You're going to rebuild our temple in *how* many days?"

They aren't expecting a deeper, change-all-the-rules, eternal truth:

"In three days I'll raise this temple, My body, from the dead to prove I'm telling the truth about Myself. I'll be doing this to demonstrate a purer, more powerful form of worship—a worship where God will no longer be living inside the temple but will actually be living inside of people."

THE REAL PROMISE

We read that Jesus finally begins to do a few miracles and, as a result, some of the people start to believe He's the Christ.

But He knows what they're really thinking. He knows that if He lets them have their way they'll try to set Him up as a political king. He knows that they don't understand the deeper type of rulership He has in mind—the rulership over people's hearts.

The same is true today. How many times have we heard people hawk Christianity as if it were Dr.

Johnson's Magic Cure-all?

Yes siree-bob, just say the magic words, "I believe," and I guarantee you more riches than you'll ever be able to spend, more joy than your circuits can handle, and so much peace and happiness, why, you'll think you've already died and gone to glory.

Then, when disaster strikes, the people feel ripped off, as if God's somehow cheated them.

But, you see, Jesus never promised that we'd be millionaires. He never promised us carefree lives without storms. And He certainly never said we'd giggle our way into heaven.

He promised us wealth, sure, but a spiritual wealth—a wealth that overflows from inside.

He promised us peace, but an inner peace that remains no matter how ugly the outward circumstances may get.

And He promised us joy—but a joy that comes from experiencing God's love.

These are the areas that Christ wants to bless and be King over.

Yes, it's true He's also in charge of outward circumstances. But first and foremost He's interested in ruling over our hearts. Once they're changed and filled, everything else is a piece of cake.

BORN AGAIN
· ·
Read JOHN 3:1-8

Now before we come down too hard on Nicodemus, keep in mind that for his whole life the guy has basically seen and thought in physical terms. Even though he's a religious leader and should have some understanding of what God does in the supernatural, he's thinking and living only in the natural. No wonder he's a little nervous when he's told he has to be "born again." He's obviously not real keen on breaking the news to his mom.

But the same is true today. We live and think so much in the natural that we find God's *supernatural* a little confusing. We wind up looking at Christianity as a religious code, full of do's and don'ts, instead of as a supernatural relationship and empowering by God.

For most of us, trying to understand this relationship and empowering is like being blind and trying to understand the concept of color. If you've never had sight, how can you understand, say, the color blue?

Just tell me what blue sounds like, OK? No? Well then, how about its taste? All right, all right—then just tell me what blue feels like.

Obviously none of these descriptions works. Sight is different from our other senses, just as touch is different from taste, hearing different from smell . . . and the spiritual different from the physical.

So Jesus tries to make it as simple to understand as possible. He explains that to enter the kingdom of God—to experience all of the Lord's gifts both now (while we're alive on earth) and later (in heaven)—

we have to be "born again."

Not a bad description. Just as we had to be born in the flesh to enter our flesh-and-bone lives, we have to be born in the Spirit to enter our spiritual lives.

But this does not happen by itself. Contrary to what New Age and Eastern mystics teach, we are *not* born "at one with God and the universe." In actuality we are born *cut off from God;* we are born spiritually unplugged from our Power Source.

Why?

Sin.

But the moment that sin is paid for, the moment we ask Jesus to be our Saviour and to come inside our lives to rule—right then—our spiritual lives are born. Those dead parts of our lives, our spirits, are suddenly energized—they suddenly come to life. Suddenly, we have entered the kingdom of heaven.

Now that doesn't mean instant maturity. When a baby is born, he or she doesn't immediately understand and function as a full-scale human. It takes time. But gradually, as we grow and feed our spirits, the spiritual things will begin to make more and more sense.

THE FINAL DECISION
. . . .
Read JOHN 3:9-21

Old Nic is still having a hard time understanding this "born again" business, so Jesus tries another approach. Since Nicodemus is a Pharisee and knows the Old Testament backward and forward, Jesus uses an example from it to try to help Nicodemus understand what He's talking about.

Back in Old Testament times (Numbers 21), when the people rebelled against God, the Lord sent a plague of poisonous snakes as punishment. The only way they could be saved from this punishment was by looking at a bronze snake Moses had made and put high up on a pole for everyone to see.

It was a simple request. All they had to do to be saved was to look at the bronze snake. Once they did, they were healed. What could be easier?

The same is true today. To be saved, all people have to do is look at Jesus. That was the whole reason He came—to save us—so of course He would make it as simple as possible.

And yet people still refuse. Why? Why, when there's a clear-cut way of getting right with God and becoming His friend, do people still ignore Him?

I suppose for some it's just a matter of ignorance. But that excuse can't last forever. God makes it crystal clear to most people who hear the Gospel that they need to receive Jesus as their Saviour.

But, according to Christ, if they continue to refuse His offer, it's really because they just *don't want* that friendship with God. They like sin too much. In fact, according to the last section of today's reading, these people actually prefer living in the darkness of sin to living in the light of God.

And, being the gentleman He is, once people have made that final decision, God will honor it . . forever.

GOD'S IN LOVE
. . . .
Read JOHN 3:22-36

Some of the Baptist's disciples are complaining that he's losing his following—that this Jesus fellow is drawing a bigger box office.

But instead of hiring an ad agency or going for higher ratings, John simply explains that this is the way it has to be.

> He must become greater; I must become less.
> (verse 30)

He also uses a beautiful analogy—one that is found throughout the New Testament. In it Jesus is referred to as a groom, and His followers, you and I, are His bride.

Think of that for a moment: God the Son wants a relationship with us that is so deep, so intimate, that it can be described as a groom who longs for his new bride. He wants to share *everything* He has with us. In fact, He's so in love that He values our lives more than His. That's why He was willing to go through the hellish agony of the cross—because of His love for us.

Talk about an intense, devoted love.

That's how special each of us is to Him. That's the type of friendship God seeks with us; that's the type of intimacy we were created for, the type of unselfish love He wants to share.

That's what we were originally created to enjoy.

And that's what He yearns and cries out for us to accept.

CHAPTER THREE

. . . .

THE REAL THING

JOHN 4–5

I'D LOVE TO JOIN YOU, STU, BUT HEY... WITH THE CHURCH'S BOWLING FOR BLESSINGS TEAM, JOGGERS FOR JESUS, AND KARATE FOR CHRIST... WELL, I'M JUST TOO BUSY SERVING GOD TO WASTE TIME PRAYING.

HOWIE MISSES THE POINT.

I'LL DRINK TO THAT
Read JOHN 4:1-26

Samaritans were considered top-of-the-line, triple-A scuzzballs. In fact the Jews hated them so much that they'd travel completely out of their way just to make sure their feet didn't touch Samaritan soil.

But not Jesus. He moves right on in. Not only does He enter their territory, but He actually strikes up a conversation with the "low-life vermin."

Unheard of! But I guess He figures scuzzballs need as much love as saints.

Not a bad lesson for us *all* to remember.

LIVING WATER

All of her life this Samaritan woman has been trying to fill up the emptiness inside her. All of her life she had been trying to quench the thirst in her soul. Like so many, she's certain that she can fill that lonely emptiness by finding the perfect relationship, by finding Mr. Right. But after six times at bat she's not any closer to getting on base than when she started.

The only thing her attempts have done is to alienate her from the rest of the people. Let's face it, after six tries this lady's got some reputation. (That's probably why she was facing the hot, midday sun instead of going to the well in the evening when things were cooler and everyone else was there.) The very thing she used to try to escape her loneliness actually made it worse.

That's the trouble with sin or anything else we use to try to replace God. It simply will not last. In fact it will eventually leave us thirstier than when we started. Oh, at first it may seem to satisfy, but eventually sin will always, *always* take more than it gives.

It's like drinking salt water. For a moment it seems to do the trick. But actually the more people drink the thirstier they become. So they keep on drinking, getting thirstier and thirstier, drinking more, getting even thirstier, and so on until finally, well, you guessed it, they die. And you know what they die of? All the salt they have taken in demands too much water for their kidneys to keep functioning. So they actually die of dehydration.

That's how sin works. It's a false satisfier that winds up killing.

But Jesus claims to be just the opposite. He says that He is "living water." He says that all we have to do is drink of Him and we'll never be thirsty again— we'll never have that deep longing that just can't seem to be satisfied. In fact He says that if we drink His water we'll have so much satisfaction, so much love, peace, and joy, that it'll actually be bubbling up from inside our souls and pouring over—as if we each had a private spring (sort of a porta-well) gurgling up inside us and always available no matter what particular desert we may find ourselves wandering through.

REAL SATISFACTION

. . . .

Read JOHN 4:27-42

When the disciples return, they're pretty amazed to see Jesus chatting away with the Samaritan woman. I mean, it was bad enough she was a Samaritan, but the fact that she was a woman made it even worse. You see, the prejudice against women was pretty strong back then. In fact the rabbis even had a saying that went, "It's better to burn the Law than give it to women."

Nice guys.

Interestingly enough, despite all the knocks it gets from the world, Christianity has done more to free women from this second-rate citizen mentality than all of the current women's movements together. In fact it was the New Testament itself that came up with the radical concept:

> There is neither Jew nor Greek, slave nor free, male nor female, for you are all one in Christ Jesus.
>
> (Galatians 3:28)

So if you've been thinking that God sees some people as better than others, think again.

REAL FOOD

When the disciples return and want to know what Jesus has eaten, He explains that His food, His real fulfillment, comes from doing the Father's work. I think it's safe to say that helping this woman at the well was more satisfying to Jesus than any number of Big Macs He could have put away.

The same is true today. There is nothing more gratifying than helping someone understand what Christ has done and encouraging that person to accept His offer. There is nothing more satisfying than helping to save someone's life—for eternity.

But today, in this age of "Whoever Dies with the Most Toys Wins," it's sometimes hard to remember where real happiness lies. It's hard not to be tricked into thinking that satisfaction comes from things. It's hard to remember that there's a deeper, more permanent joy—a joy that comes from friendship with God and from loving and serving His children.

Love and *service*—that's our real food, our real satisfaction.

If you're trying to decide what to do with your life, don't forget to check with God. See what way He'd like you to be in service for Him. Now it's true that you may not get the house on the lake, the European vacations, or even that BMW. But you'll be getting a deeper satisfaction, a satisfaction that the others, with their toys, can never achieve.

Today, more than ever, the fields really are "ripe for harvest." There are millions who have never even heard the name of Jesus. There is an entire world out there (and in your own backyard) that is sick and hungry and just generally beaten up. A world that is literally going to hell. The question is:

Does God want you to help?

It won't always be easy, it won't always be fun and games . . . but it will always be an adventure.

And the benefits? Well, let's just say the dividends are definitely out of this world.

LONG-DISTANCE HEALING
Read JOHN 4:43-54

Lots of people think that healings back in Jesus' day and even in ours are just basically mind over matter. A person wants to be healed so badly or gets so worked up emotionally that his mind makes the healing happen.

But nothing could be further from the truth for this official's son. Let's face it, the poor kid doesn't even know what's going on. Here he lies, sick and dying in Capernaum, when all the way over at Cana Jesus says he's healed.

The kid isn't doing anything, he doesn't hear anything, he isn't at some "faith rally" getting all worked up and screaming, "I believe, I believe." He just lies there, dying—until Jesus says, "You will live."

The same thing happened to me a few years back (but not nearly as dramatically). Until that time I had always secretly thought that people who got healed were never really sick. Either that or they just worked themselves up into such a frenzy that somehow their minds did it. But for God just to do it on His own—I mean, get real.

My thoughts have changed.

I was asked to go to a service a well-known musician friend was leading about 10 miles from my house. But earlier that afternoon I had sprained my left ankle. And because I had hurt it while doing something for the Lord, I was mad and decided just to stay home and pout. That ought to show God.

Anyway, at about 8:30 that evening I noticed the pain in my ankle had stopped. I began walking on it, then running, and finally jumping—thinking, "That's weird, I was so sure there was something wrong. Oh well. . . ."

It wasn't until a couple of days later that I found out what had really happened. It seemed that in the middle of his song my friend felt that a bunch of healings were taking place and started naming them off. By the end of the service every one of those healings had happened and every one was accounted for . . . except, of course, for one. It seems no one there had a sprained left ankle.

And the time all of this was going on? You guessed it—8:30.

It was then that I finally got around to learning what the Bible already teaches. God doesn't need our help to perform His miracles. He doesn't need us to get all worked up and emotionally hyped.

Miracles are not mind over matter. They are God over matter. Sometimes they happen; sometimes they don't. But the point is they're inspired by God—not man.

A DIFFERENT SET OF RULES

Read JOHN 5:1-15

Life must be pretty miserable for this guy. Here he is, unable to walk, crowded in with the rest of the city's suffering—his only goal to fight and scratch and claw to be the first into the pool to get healed. And to top it off he's been doing this for 38 years and still hasn't succeeded!

Talk about a loser life.

But in some ways is that life any different from our lives today? Now granted, we may not have some fancy healing pool to fight and claw to get to—but today, in this pressure-cooker world of ours, we certainly have enough other competitions: *I've got to get better grades so I can get into a better school, so I can get a better job, so I can get better money, so I can have a better life.*

Or, for those of us who think in short-range terms: *I've got to get that parking spot before he does!*

Whatever our goals, we are all living in a pressure-cooker world—a world *full* of competition. It's a hard, vicious, exhausting game. Forget about being a superstar—for most of us just trying to get on the scoreboard is tough enough.

But the good news is we don't have to score points. In fact we don't even have to play the game.

But if I don't score more points than What's-His-Face, then What's-His-Face'll get all the prizes.

He might. But so will you—*if you put Christ first.*

But seek first His kingdom and His righteousness, and all these things will be given to you as well.
(Matthew 6:33)

Now that doesn't mean that by putting Christ first you magically breeze through your SATs, cruise into Harvard, become president of IBM, and make your first million by age 20. But it does mean that Jesus will specifically pick *you* out of the crowd (just as He did the lame man), and give you the wholeness and happiness you *really* want. If being rich will do it, then rich you will be. But chances are He'll be giving you a deeper and more lasting happiness— one that most billionaires will never have.

The important thing is that you don't have to claw your way to the top. All you have to do is obey.

I'll never forget when I was a little guy watching a parade. The clowns were throwing handfuls of candy on the street, and all the kids were racing out, pushing and shoving to get a piece or two. All the kids but me; my parents wouldn't let me take part in the mayhem.

Talk about a ruined day. Didn't they understand? How could I be happy and get the stuff everybody else had if I didn't fight for it?

But from high atop the float, one of the clowns noticed my grudging obedience to my parents. And to this day I'll never forget what he did. Old Bozo hopped off the float, waded through the crowd, and, to everybody's amazement, dropped a huge handful of candy right into my lap.

Now I did nothing to earn that candy. All I did was stay at my parents' side. All I did was obey.

The same is true for us today. While the rest of the world is kicking and fighting and scrambling, all we need to do is rest in the Lord. Refuse to be sucked into that hectic, frenzied, me-first thinking. Make your priority to seek Jesus and obey; after that, the *real* prizes will just fall into your lap.

You have my word on it. Better yet, you have His.

RADICAL CLAIMS
. . . .
Read JOHN 5:16-30

The religious hotshots are complaining that Jesus broke the Sabbath by healing the guy at the pool. Jesus blows them away by saying, "Hey look, My Father does good on the Sabbath, so why shouldn't I? If it's good enough for God, it's good enough for Me."

This raises everyone's blood pressure a few dozen points because it's pretty obvious that Jesus is making Himself out to be equal with God. And just to make sure there's no mistake about it, He goes on to make a few other spectacular claims:

- The Father shows Jesus everything He does (verse 20).
- Jesus can give eternal life to whomever He wants (verse 21).
- The Father has given *all* authority of judging the world to Jesus (verse 22).
- Anyone who hears and believes Jesus will live forever (verse 24).

Now these are some pretty radical claims. No wonder the people are trying to kill Him. But the greatest claim comes in verse 23:

> He who does not honor the Son does not honor the Father, who sent Him.

Quite a statement . . . and a pretty clear answer to the following argument:

Hey, don't get me wrong. I believe in a God out there somewhere. I mean, I'm no atheist or anything like that. I just don't buy all this Jesus junk.

That may be so. But the problem is that you can't have one without the other. They're interconnected. The only way we can honor God is if we honor His Son.

In other words . . .

If we reject Jesus—we reject God.

If we accept Jesus—we accept God.

. . . He gives us no other alternative.

RELIGION VS. RELATIONSHIP

Read JOHN 5:31-47

Some people will do anything they can *not* to surrender their life to Christ . . . EVEN IF IT MEANS BECOMING A CHRISTIAN.

The energized, overflowing life Jesus is always talking about lies in Him. It does not lie in Bible studies; it does not lie in Sunday School, youth group, choir practice, or sacrificial service to others. It doesn't even lie in going to church!

Now don't get me wrong: these things are all important. They all help draw us closer to Him. But many people use all of this busyness as an excuse NOT to give themselves to Him. Instead of quietly seeking Him with a sincere heart that says, "Whatever You want, it's Yours," they get all involved in "works" so they can give Him just what *they* want to give.

In essence that's what's happening in this section of John's account. All of these scholars have been carefully studying God's Word and the writings of Moses. By doing all of this religious work they think they're getting eternal life.

But Jesus comes flat out and says, "No way. All these things testify about Me and speak about Me— but they are NOT ME. And the *Me* part, that personal relationship with *Me*, that's what's going to save you; that's where real life is."

The same is true today. We can get so caught up in all of the religious things to say and do that we forget the one Person they're all pointing to. Or, worse yet, we use them as an excuse *not* to get real with Him—to prevent Him from really touching our hearts.

Sometimes we're like the parents who are so busy earning money to buy stuff for their kids that they never take time to give the kids what they really want—they never give them their love.

God does not want our sacrifice—He wants our love. God does not want our works—He wants our hearts.

CHAPTER FOUR

. . . .

GOING ALL THE WAY
JOHN 6

HOWIE SUSPECTS THAT WALKING ON WATER MIGHT BE A MINOR MIRACLE BY COMPARISON.

GOING FOR BROKE
. . . .
Read JOHN 6:1-14

A hefty crowd is starting to follow Jesus. And in this section it looks like He can't even get a few minutes alone with His disciples before the groupies start closing in.

Now Jesus has been pretty busy in the miracle department and so far He seems to be batting about 1.000. So you'd think His question to the disciples about how to feed all the people wouldn't have been too tough to answer.

Well, not exactly.

Let's take a look at three responses to this question:

PHILIP

First of all there was Philip. Like so many of us, he forgets what Jesus has done in the past. He forgets how much the Lord wants to bless us. Instead he looks at the situation and panics: "Even if we scraped up eight months' wages, we couldn't feed this mob!"

OK . . . thanks for sharing, Phil.

ANDREW

Then there's Andrew, doing what he does best: bringing people to Jesus. Remember how he ran out and brought his brother, Peter, to Him?

This time he's bringing a little boy with a few crumby loaves and a couple of fish. He's not sure *how,* or even *if*—but there's something inside him that figures Jesus *might* be able to pull this one off. It's as if there's this tiny little kernel of faith. Still, his response, "But how far will they go?" makes it pretty clear that he's not totally sold.

LITTLE BOY

Finally, there's the little boy. Now, it's a safe guess that the bread and fish were for his lunch—and they weren't much. The loaves were small, and scholars believe the fish were pickled and about the size of sardines.

But instead of hoarding the food and keeping it for himself, he volunteered to give it all away. He trusted Jesus enough to give Him all that he had.

And the result? Five thousand men (not to mention all the women and children) ate as much as they wanted, leaving 12 baskets full of leftovers! Not a bad return on the boy's investment.

Isn't this third response, this boy's action, exactly what God wants from us? Doesn't He want us to go for broke? To put all of our eggs into His basket? To put everything that we have into His hands?

It's certainly not mandatory. We can hold back— make sure we have enough for ourselves, and then maybe, *maybe* give Him a little of the leftovers. But look at the excitement and joy the boy would have missed if he had made that choice. Look at the selfish, boring day he would have had.

And, today, look at the selfish, boring lives of Christians who maybe give God a little but refuse to trust Him all the way.

Now granted, it takes courage to trust God—to give Him all that we have. But it's like any other investment. The more we give, the more we receive. And by giving Him more and more of our lives, we

get more and more of His all-powerful life.
Not a bad trade-off.

GOD'S CARE
Read JOHN 6:15-21

Suddenly we see the people planning to take Jesus by force so they can make Him King. Why?

They want to use Him.

USING GOD

For years the Jews had been forced to live under Roman rule. (It would be the same as if Russia had invaded our country and we had to live under Moscow rule.) You can understand why, after seeing all His miracles, the Jews think they can use Jesus to do a little Roman-bashing.

But Jesus will not be manipulated. God wants to give us overflowing life, sure, but on *His* terms, not ours. He wants to save these people, yes, but He wants to save them from eternal death and hell, not from the Romans. He wants to give them what they *really* need, not what they think they want.

And look at what He does when they try to force Him to play by their rules. He just sort of . . . disappears.

That's worth keeping in mind. The next time we try to manipulate and con God into letting us have our own, narrow-minded, little ways, let's not be too surprised if suddenly, in those particular situations . . . He's not so easy to find.

DON'T BE AFRAID

It's been only a few hours since the miracle with the bread and fish. But already the disciples are having a rough go of it. They're in the middle of a storm, three and a half miles from shore, in the dead of night, when, suddenly, they see Jesus walking on the water toward them.

Their response? Not exactly a 10 on the Richter scale of faith. Instead of saying, "Lord, once again we see You're who You claim to be and thank You for coming to save us," they freak.

But Jesus' words calm and quiet them: "It is I, don't be afraid" (verse 20).

This same Jesus who walked out on the people trying to manipulate Him, walked *in* on His disciples who really needed Him.

What a comfort it is to know that no matter what situation we may find ourselves in, no matter how frightened we are—what a comfort to know He's always there. Not to tell us we're jerks for getting caught in the storm, not to yell at us for having so little faith. Instead, He's always there to watch over us, to encourage us, to ease our fears. He is always there, willing to climb into our boats and weather our storms . . . with us.

BREAD OF LIFE
. . . .
Read JOHN 6:22-40

The next morning the crowd, wondering what the Great Caterer from Heaven has for breakfast, starts looking for Him. They know the disciples left the night before without Jesus, and they know there were no other boats, so they're having a bit of a problem figuring out exactly how He slipped past them.

When they finally do catch up, Jesus points out that they really didn't search for Him because of the miracles—they came because they ate the bread He'd provided and were filled.

But He explains that, even though they were satisfied by the bread, they shouldn't be so concerned about physical food. It spoils. He has a different type of food, a food for the soul that satisfies a deeper hunger—a food that satisfies the hunger for love, for truth, for fulfillment.

And, most important, He points out that it is a food only *He* can provide.

REAL WORK

The people immediately want to know what they can do to earn this love, this fulfilled life. In short, they want to know what they can do to earn God's favor. Jesus' answer couldn't be simpler:

"Believe in Me."

"Fine," they say. "If you want us to believe in You, then show us a sign." (As if He hadn't shown them enough already.) "You've fed us only one meal— Moses gave our ancestors bread from heaven every

51

day for 40 years. Top that, Hotshot."

Not only can Jesus top it—He says He is "it."

> I am the Bread of Life. He who comes to Me will never go hungry, and he who believes in Me will never be thirsty.
>
> (verse 35)

EATING AND DRINKING CHRIST
Read JOHN 6:41-59

The people start complaining, "Hey, we knew this guy when He was in Pampers. Where does He come off with this 'I'm heaven-sent' stuff? Who does He think He is, anyway?"

Instead of trying to convince them, Jesus tells them to relax. Nothing He can say or do will convince them. If they're really listening to God, then God is the one who'll let them know.

> Everyone who listens to the Father and learns from Him comes to Me.
>
> (verse 45)

The same is true today. If people are sincerely looking, God will show them.

EAT MY FLESH—DRINK MY BLOOD

This is one of the most important instructions to Christians in the entire Bible. But more than a few people have completely misunderstood it. In fact some have even accused Christians of being cannibals. What they don't understand is that this is the number one ingredient in the life of any believer in Jesus Christ.

As a human I am made up of amino acids, water, minerals, and so on. For the most part I cannot manufacture these ingredients on my own. I need to take them into my system. I need to eat them. If I do, I live. If I don't, I die.

The same is true with our spiritual natures. We

cannot manufacture spiritual ingredients on our own. To survive spiritually, we have to eat spiritual food. And that's what Jesus claims to be.

Our spiritual food is not in church services, Sunday School, religious works, or even being "a good Christian." It is in Jesus Christ.

We have to spiritually eat Him. We have to digest Him and allow Him to become incorporated into our spiritual beings. He wants to draw so close and love us so deeply that He actually starts to become a part of us. And it is that oneness that gives us overwhelming love, peace, and joy. It is that oneness that gives us the "abundant life" He keeps promising.

But if we refuse, if we don't eat His body and drink His blood—if we refuse to commune and have fellowship with Him—the only thing waiting for us is spiritual starvation.

And with starvation . . . eventually comes death.

ALL OR NOTHING
. . . .
Read JOHN 6:60-71

This is one of the greatest tests in Jesus' life. The crowds are growing. They're following Him wherever He goes. In fact, as we've read, they're even planning on making Him King.

Talk about an opportunity. By just keeping His mouth shut He can have all the power, fame, and riches that others only dream about. By not telling the whole truth, by candy-coating it ever so slightly, He can have everybody following Him.

But Jesus is not after numbers. He's not interested in quantity, He's interested in quality. If it means only 12 men and a few women following Him then so be it—but those few will be *entirely* committed. They won't be fence sitters. They won't be people who are kind of into Jesus and kind of into the world. They will be people totally sold on Him.

The same is true today. God doesn't ask us to add a little of Himself into our lives—He asks to *become* our lives. He's not interested in people who dabble at Jesus—He's interested in people who *live* Jesus.

I once drew a thermometer and asked members from a youth group to tell me what temperatures they felt best represented their spiritual lives. No one picked too cold and no one picked too hot. Instead nearly everyone picked the nice, safe, mid-70s.

Then I asked them to turn to Revelation 3:15-16. It's a letter Jesus dictated to a bunch of Christians in Laodicea:

I know your deeds, that you are neither cold nor

hot. I wish you were either one or the other! So, because you are lukewarm—neither hot nor cold—I am about to spit you out of My mouth.

Needless to say there were a couple uncomfortable moments in the group.

The point is that Jesus is not interested in people who play church. He's interested in people who *are* the church—people who are a living, breathing, loving part of His body—people who are totally committed to Him.

Now that doesn't mean we're perfect! And it certainly doesn't mean we're always able to put Him first. It just means we *want* to. (Or at least want to want to.)

Because if we're not interested in putting Him first, then maybe we're just fooling ourselves. Maybe we're like the multitudes that were just hanging around for another free meal, or because that's where their friends were, or because they wanted to use Jesus for selfish motives.

If that's the case, then maybe we should move on and stop playing church.

There's just one little problem. Simon Peter saw it, and it's just as true today as it was then:

Lord, to whom shall we go? You have the words of eternal life.

(John 6:68)

CHAPTER FIVE

DECISIONS

JOHN 7–8

HOWIE CASTS THE FIRST STONE.

TRUE JUDGMENT

Read JOHN 7:1-24

The Feast of Tabernacles is coming up. This is a big, eight-day celebration in mid-October that, among other things, is kind of like our Thanksgiving. Anybody who's anybody tries to make it to Jerusalem for the good times.

So Jesus' brothers begin taunting Him. "Hey listen, Mr. Miracles. You think You're so special, then head on up to Jerusalem. Let everyone see what a big man You are with Your fancy little magic tricks!"

But just as before, Jesus isn't letting anyone force His hand. He's going, all right, but on His terms—not at the beginning, but later on when the party's in full swing.

By the time He arrives (incognito), He's already the talk of the town (or whisper of the town, since everybody's afraid to speak up because of the religious leaders). Some of the people are saying He's a "good man"—others are saying He's a trickster. Interestingly, no one is paying any attention to who He says He is.

Too bad. (Yet I wonder how different that is from today.)

About halfway through the festival Jesus finally makes His appearance at the temple court (the very center of the Jewish religion). He begins to teach, and the bigwigs are pretty impressed. They want to know how He got so smart without attending Jerusalem U.

"My teaching is not My own," Jesus replies. "It comes from Him who sent Me!" (verse 16)

Figuring this is going to create the usual problems, He again tells them to check out His credentials. "Ask God—see if I'm for real. And if I am for real, then ask yourself why you're trying to kill Me."

"You're crackers!" they shout. "No one's trying to kill You!"

Knowing better, Jesus continues:

"I did one miracle on the Sabbath (the healing of the man at the pool) and you're all hot and bothered. Everyone's bent out of shape because I helped some poor guy who'd been suffering for years. Yet you circumcise babies on this very same day! Tell Me, what's more important—following some religious ritual of circumcision or loving and healing a human being?

"Stop being so legalistic! Look at the whole picture. Don't judge by outward appearances. Get *all* the facts. If you're going to judge, at least get help from the Final Authority!"

THINGS HEAT UP
. . . .
Read JOHN 7:25-53

The people finally catch on that Jesus is the one everyone's been talking about. But to realize it's Jesus is one thing. To actually believe He's Christ . . . well now, that's another.

"Besides," they say, "everybody knows where this guy's from—when the Christ comes no one will know where He's from."

(Not exactly true. Most everyone and his brother knew the prophecy in Micah 5:2 that said the Christ would be born in Bethlehem.)

But right now Jesus isn't particularly interested in going through His life history; He's interested in preaching the truth and helping people.

Unfortunately, people like help, but the truth part, especially when it's directed at their personal lives, can make them a little irritable—as seen here where they go for Jesus' throat when He points out that they don't really know God.

But because "His time had not yet come" (verse 30), they can't touch Him.

The same thing happens when the Pharisees send out guards to arrest Him. For some reason they don't grab Him. Instead, they wind up listening.

But the good times won't last forever. Jesus explains that pretty soon He'll be taking off and heading back to "the One who sent Me" (verse 33).

LIVING SPRINGS

As part of the ceremony of the Feast of Tabernacles, the priest pours water on the temple altar while the people shout praises to God. It's quite a spectacle and designed in part to thank the Lord for His life-giving gift of water.

Everybody's into the celebration when suddenly Jesus stands up and shouts, "If anyone is thirsty, let him come to *Me* and drink. Whoever believes in *Me*, as the Scripture has said, streams of living water will flow from within him" (verses 37-38, italics added).

No doubt that puts a little crimp in the ceremony. Not only is Jesus interrupting the proceedings, but He's claiming to be the source of something far more real and far more important than what they're currently praising God for.

THE REAL REASON

In this final section we again see how much the Pharisees hate Jesus. But why? What's the big deal? It's got to be more than the fact that He's interrupted a ceremony or two. If they think He's a madman, why not just have Him committed? If they think He's a con artist, just expose Him and lock Him up. And if He really is who He says He is, then they should be out of their minds with joy—I mean, if this is the One they've been waiting for all these years, it should be "Hallelujah Chorus" time!

Unfortunately, the same reason they hated Jesus back then is the same reason a lot of people hate and refuse Him today. It has nothing to do with clear thinking or logic. It doesn't even have to do with proof. (As we'll discuss later, there are all sorts of proof available for anyone who wants to do a little research.)

No, the real reason people reject Christ has nothing to do with proof or logic. The real reason has to do with their *wills.*

To acknowledge Jesus Christ as Lord would mean:

1. Having an authority higher than themselves. It would mean they could no longer run their own lives and live under their own sets of rules. They would have to submit their wills to somebody else's; they would have to let God call the shots.

2. Being humbled. They would have to admit that all of their education and intellect are of no help. The only way they can get into heaven is the old-fashioned way. They have to rely on Christ.

3. Change of lifestyle. They would have to clean up their acts and obey God.

These are the real reasons people reject Christ. It has nothing to do with proof. It has everything to do with who they want to be "The Boss."

THE PERFECT TRAP—ALMOST
Read JOHN 8:1-11

The following morning, Jesus is again teaching at the temple. Only this time He's sitting down and the atmosphere is a lot more relaxed . . . until the Pharisees drag in some poor woman caught in adultery.

Talk about having Jesus cornered. Here He's been doing all of this teaching about God's love and how He wants to give us life. And now suddenly the religious leaders confront Him with somebody that according to Old Testament Law should actually be executed!

What can He do? If He says, "Stone her," all of His talk about love and forgiveness will be a joke.

If He says, "Let her go," He'll be saying God's Word is a joke.

From every angle it looks like they finally have Him trapped.

But Jesus will not be put in a box. They've given Him two choices to choose from. So what does He do? He picks a third. (How many times in our own lives have we asked God, "All right, which is it, choice A or choice B?" and seen Him come up with choice W?)

"OK, you want to kill her?" Jesus says. "Then kill her. But, oh, by the way . . . just make sure that the first one to start the execution isn't guilty of anything himself."

What a phenomenal answer! Once again He's turned a religious, self-righteous group around and forced them to look at their own hearts. And it looks like they're not too thrilled with what they see.

To this day no one's sure what Jesus wrote when

He bent down and scribbled on the ground. Some think it was a list of each of the Pharisees' sins. Whatever it was, the accusers began to leave—the oldest first (they have more sins to remember) on down to the youngest.

Once again we see the other side of Jesus' love— the tender, gentle side that wants to forgive sins. I know we've heard this a billion times before, but just stop and think about it a minute.

It makes no difference what we've done. It doesn't even matter if, as in the woman's case, our sin is worthy of the death penalty. The point is:

Jesus wants to forgive us of all that we've ever done wrong.

Talk about freedom! Imagine knowing that whenever we foul up, whenever we make a mistake, Jesus is there to forgive us. He's always there to pick us up and help us get back on our feet, just as He did with this woman.

And look how He does it. He doesn't clobber her over the head with guilt. He doesn't go around sulking, holding it above her, or trying to make her feel like beetle spit. He just gently and tenderly tells her she's forgiven. That's it, end of discussion.

Oh, there's one other thing Jesus says that we should keep in mind—His last words to the woman:

"Sin no more" (John 8:11, NASB).

TOTAL FREEDOM

Read JOHN 8:12-41

Once again Jesus is coming down pretty hard on all the religious bigwigs. Quite a contrast to how kind and gentle He was with the woman who had committed adultery.

Why? What's the difference?

And, most important, how can we make sure He responds to us the way He did to the woman and not the way He did to the Pharisees?

As usual, the answer has to do with our hearts. If we're self-righteous and think we have it all together, or if we think that we're better than the next person, Jesus' response to us will probably be the same as it was to the Pharisees.

Why?

Because we're lying to ourselves. We think we really don't need God. We think we can make it on our own "goodness." So Jesus has to shatter our little fantasy worlds and show us what we're *really* like so we'll turn to Him for help.

The woman caught in adultery already knew she needed help. Inside she was already crying out to be saved. It was that crying out that Jesus responded to.

The key is to save Jesus (and ourselves) that first step, that "shattering process." The key is to stand before Him with our arms already reaching out for help . . . not folded across our chests in smug piety.

SLAVES OF SIN

Some of the people are starting to believe in Jesus, so He gives them a little more truth.

"Everyone who sins is a slave to sin" (verse 34).

Of course this gets everyone riled. (Funny, they were so comfortable when the Pharisees were under the gun.)

Once again Jesus is delivering some hard-hitting truth. Sin is deceptive. On the outside it usually looks great—lots of fun and grins—a shortcut to good times.

The problem is, underneath all that flashy, good-times bait, there lies a hook. Oh, we may not feel it at first. In fact the bait may be so tasty that we just keep on chowing down. But eventually, somewhere along the line, we run into the hook. And gradually, *without our even knowing it,* that hook starts to dig in—*without our even knowing it,* it starts to control . . . and there's nothing we can do about it. It makes no difference how smart or careful we are; if we're nibbling on sin, we'll become its slave.

It can be anything—sex, drugs, lying, cheating, gossiping, materialism, self-centeredness—you name it, once we take the bait, it takes control.

But the good news is Jesus can break that control. He says He can free us. Don't ask me how. I've never been able to figure that part out. But I've seen it happen in my own life a hundred times. Somehow, as we give Him control of our lives and spend time with Him, the old desires and enslavements just sort of fade away.

It doesn't always happen overnight. But if we're really honest in pursuing Him, if we're *really* honest in wanting to be free of the sin, He'll be there to break its grip and set us free.

It's true: not only does Jesus forgive us when we sin, but He actually gives us the power to stop sinning.

A LITTLE SHAKE-UP
. . . .
Read JOHN 8:42-59

I used to think Jesus was this mild-mannered little guy who had nothing but hugs and "love ya's" for everybody. But according to today's section that's not exactly the case:

You do not belong to God.

(verse 47)

You belong to your father, the devil.

(verse 44)

Let's face it, He's definitely not going to be named Mr. Congeniality. But it's this next verse that really shakes the people up:

I tell you the truth, If anyone keeps My word he will never see death.

(verse 51)

"Now we know You've got a screw loose!" the people shout. "Abraham died. All the great men of God died. Where do You come off saying You're better than all of them? Who do You think You are, anyway?"

Jesus' reply causes more than a few jaws to drop:

"This Abraham you make such a big deal out of, he and I actually spent some time together. And you know something else? He was thrilled about it!"

By now everyone's heart rate's up a few hundred beats. "You're not even 50 years old!" they shout. "Abraham lived 2,000 years ago!"

And Jesus' response?

"Before Abraham was born, I am!" (verse 58)

Now, not only was Jesus claiming to have lived before Abraham, but by using the phrase "I am," He was using the exact name God called Himself back in the Book of Exodus—back when Moses asked Him what He should be called.

> This is what you are to say to the Israelites: "I AM has sent me to you."
>
> (Exodus 3:14)

So if Jesus is speaking Hebrew, He's actually calling Himself by the same name God had used to identify Himself to Moses.

No wonder everyone's trying to kill Him. They know exactly what He's saying. They know exactly who He's claiming to be!

· ·

CHAPTER SIX

THE WAY IT IS

JOHN 9–10

HOWIE STUMBLES ONTO A DEEP
THEOLOGICAL TRUTH.

OUR PART
. . . .
Read JOHN 9:1-12

Once again Jesus is making a pretty hefty claim: "I am the light of the world" (verse 5). And once again we see He has the power to back it up. Any crazy can claim to be God's gift to the human race—but how many can prove it by giving sight to someone who has *never* seen?

Of course, the method may seem a little weird . . . spit pies would not have been my first choice in treatment. But keep in mind that customs back then were a little different than today. In fact people actually believed there were medicinal properties in the spit of holy men (another reason to thank God we live in this century).

Now Jesus is no idiot. He probably has a pretty good idea that spit and mud aren't going to give anyone back his sight. But He uses this backward medical practice as something the man can cling to—a security blanket to help the man's frail faith.

But in His love for the man, Jesus does not stop there. He knows that the fellow's faith needs more developing, so He challenges it again, forcing it to grow by sending him across town to wash off the mud.

Let's face it, walking through town with a spit-and-mud pie dripping down your face would be a bit of a stretch for anybody's faith. But the man continued to obey and his faith continued to grow. And by the end of this little exercise in faith, he could see!

What's this got to do with us?

You and I may not have much faith. Some of us may barely believe in Jesus. But if we're willing to obey and exercise what little faith we do have—Jesus will work with us. In fact that's part of who He is, "the author and perfecter of our faith" (Hebrews 12:2).

If we're willing to obey and believe as much as we can, Jesus will personally work with us until, just as with the blind man, our vision (of who God is and what He wants to do in our lives) will become crystal clear.

THE BLIND SEE—
THE SEEING DON'T

. . . .

Read JOHN 9:13-41

If the phrase "Don't confuse me with the facts" ever applied to anyone, it would have to be the Pharisees. Nothing could be plainer. All the witnesses agree. This man was born blind and now, thanks to Jesus, he sees. But the Pharisees aren't interested in the facts—their minds are already made up.

First they interview the man. Then his parents. Then back to the man again. The truth couldn't be clearer. But they keep right on asking until finally it gets to be such a joke that the man asks, "How many times do you have to hear this? What's the deal—are you thinking of becoming His disciples too?"

Of course they hit the ceiling. They call him a filthy sinner, pat themselves on the back for being so holy, and finally, for good measure, throw him out of their religion.

Poor guy. First he staggers around town with a mud compress, then he receives sight for the very first time, then he's interrogated by the Pharisees, and finally, to top it off, he's excommunicated (which, in his culture, not only isolates him from his faith, family, and friends, but also makes finding any type of work close to impossible).

Talk about having "one of those days." But it should be a real encouragement for us to see that Jesus doesn't desert the man. He makes a point of searching him out again and continues to help.

God is never done working with us. Even when we think He's done enough, He's always there at our sides, always ready to keep on helping, encouraging, and reaching out.

And the man's response?

Here was a guy who started out needing so much help in the faith department that Jesus had to resort to some superstitious medical practice. But by the end of the day this same guy is not only seeing and believing in Jesus, but, according to verse 38, he's one of the first ever to worship Him!

Pretty impressive growth. And all because Jesus stayed with him throughout the process . . . just as He does with us in whatever particular areas we're growing in. There may be times we think we're alone (just like when the man was being grilled by the Pharisees) but the bottom line is, He'll always be at our sides helping us to see and grow.

And the Pharisees?

Well, just as Jesus' love and truth opened the blind man's eyes, it has closed and blinded those who pride themselves on seeing.

THE GOOD SHEPHERD
. . . .
Read JOHN 10:1-21

There is no better picture of Jesus' deep love and total commitment to us than His example of being our Shepherd. To get the full scope of what He's talking about, keep in mind that the life of a dedicated shepherd meant total devotion to his flock—a devotion that included putting the sheep's lives above his.

First of all, there were thieves and robbers—dishonest men who would try to lure and steal stray lambs. They weren't interested in the animals' welfare; they were only interested in the money they could get from them.

Sound familiar? Unfortunately there's more than a few of those folks around today—people who have turned Christianity into the business of bucks instead of the commitment of love.

But Jesus makes it clear that if we honestly seek God, we'll eventually be able to tell His voice from the crooks'.

Second, there were plenty of wild animals back then—mostly wolves. Whenever they closed in, fierce and ravenous from hunger, the hired hands usually split. Why should they risk their lives for somebody else's property?

But the committed shepherd never looked upon his flock as "property." He had grown to know and love each of them as individuals. In fact, his love and dedication to them was so intense that he would actually fight to the death to protect them.

Then there was the hazardous terrain on which the sheep grazed—a dangerous landscape of holes, cliffs, and ravines. Knowing these pitfalls, the caring shepherd would never push or drive his flock. Instead he would walk ahead of them, carefully scouting out the safest routes—gently leading them in areas he had already checked out . . . at the risk of his own life.

Good pasture was also important. Grazing was about the only thing the sheep did, so why not make it as pleasant for them as possible? A sensitive shepherd would go to great risks to find the best grazing land for his sheep—to make their lives as happy and full as possible.

And finally there were the hillside pens—places where the animals could gather for protection during the night.

To make sure the sheep were really safe, the shepherd would sleep on the ground at the entrance of the pen. He would literally act as a human gate—a gate that would serve as the only means to reach the flock.

So by comparing Himself to a shepherd, this is the tender, intense, all-giving love the Lord promises:
- He will protect us from evil.
- He will fight off any enemy that's trying to destroy us.
- He will go before us in every situation.
- He will give us a happy and full life.

And He will lay down His own life for ours.
That's a committed shepherd. That's our Lord.

THE FACTS
. . . .
Read JOHN 10:22-42

This section gives more evidence of Jesus' phenomenal patience. Here He is, healing all types of people,
performing all types of miracles, and making it super
clear to the folks that He is God, the Son.

So what do they ask?

"How long are You going to keep us in sus-
pense—just tell us who You are."

Come on, guys. . . .

Once again Jesus has to make it clear that it really
doesn't matter if they have all the facts. The only
ones that are going to believe are the ones that really want to follow God. It's a matter of obedience,
not logic.

But to prove His point He goes ahead and tells
them not once, but twice, who He is. And, sure
enough, instead of dropping to their knees and crying, "We understand, forgive us," they try to kill
Him—not once, but twice.

Sadly, as we've said before, the same is true today.
Despite what people say, most really aren't looking
for proof. If they were really sincere, they could
seek God, as Jesus suggested, and find out for themselves.

And if they can't reach God, there's always the
public library.

Say what?

That's right. You see, there are hundreds of books
that scientifically, historically, archeologically, and
even mathematically show that Christ had to be who
He said He was. In fact several authors who have set
out to disprove Christ have, by the end of their

research, actually become Christians.

Instead of boring you with a long list of books, let me recommend just one for starters. *Evidence That Demands a Verdict,* by Josh McDowell (published by Campus Crusade for Christ), is a thorough reference book that covers a lot of the facts demonstrating the truth of the Bible and Jesus Christ.

The facts are available for anyone who's really interested. It isn't a lack of facts that prevents people from receiving Jesus Christ.

No, today, just as it was back then, the problem is not with the facts. The problem is with the human will.

CHAPTER SEVEN

ARISE!

JOHN 11

NOW, LET ME GET THIS STRAIGHT. YOU ASKED GOD TO DELIVER A DOUBLE-SPACED, TYPED TERM PAPER ON THE POETRY OF ROBERT FROST TO YOUR LOCKER FIVE MINUTES BEFORE CLASS STARTS?!

HOWIE DISCOVERS HOW NOT TO WAIT ON THE LORD.

WAIT ON THE LORD
Read JOHN 11:1-16

Lazarus and Jesus were the best of buddies. And since Jesus was always showing His love for others, and since the two were such good friends, Martha and Mary just naturally figured Jesus would race to their brother's aid.

Not quite.

Instead, Jesus waits a few more days until Lazarus is good and dead.

Why? I thought He loved Lazarus. If God, who's supposed to love everybody, treats His best friends this way, how can we expect to be treated any differently?

We can't. But here's something we *can* expect . . .

I tell you the truth, My Father will give you whatever you ask in My name. Until now you have not asked for anything in My name. Ask and you will receive, and your joy will be complete.

(John 16:23-24)

God wants to bless us, usually more than we can imagine. But often, especially when we're young, our timetable is radically different from His. We're out there wanting to Grand Prix it, to get everything now while the getting's good. Meanwhile God's out there saying, "Hold on a minute. If you just wait another second and leave it to Me, I'll make it better."

Unfortunately, by not waiting we usually wind up with *our* second rate instead of *God's* first rate. Instead of waiting on His time schedule so the fruit

80

can ripen and sweeten, our fears and impatience tell us to grab it now when it's still green and bitter.

We keep forgetting that God sees the whole picture—that He knows the precise day of picking. He knows when that fruit we want so desperately will be at its peak. If we let Him, He'll always wait until the perfect moment before harvesting that fruit and answering our prayers. Never a minute too early—never a minute too late.

Let's face it, by going on Jesus' timetable Mary and Martha are definitely going to have a little more spice in their lives than if they could have forced God to follow their own schedule!

The same is true for us. There are times when it seems like God has completely missed the boat. There are times when our hopes and dreams seem totally dead. But if we wait on Him, our experience will be the same as Lazarus'.

If we wait on Him, we'll wind up with greater life than we could possibly have expected.

> Yet those who wait for the Lord will gain new strength;
> They will mount up with wings like eagles,
> They will run and not get tired,
> They will walk and not become weary.
>
> (Isaiah 40:31, NASB)

Waiting isn't always the easiest—but if it's what God wants, it will always be the best.

GOD CRIES

Read JOHN 11:17-37

Once again Jesus makes a startling claim:

I am the resurrection and the life. He who believes in Me will live, even though he dies; and whoever lives and believes in Me will never die.
(verses 25-26)

Notice, He doesn't say, "I'll show you the way to live so you won't die," or, "If you follow My teachings, you'll have eternal life." Instead He says *He* is that life—*He* is that resurrection!

Jesus is not offering a new set of rules or a new religion. He is offering a *relationship*—a relationship with Himself. *He* is the "bread of life," *He* is the "living water," *He* is the "resurrection and the life."

To try to get those things on our own by being extra good or religious would be as stupid as an empty baseball glove trying to play center field on its own. It can be flapping around out there all it wants, but it's not likely to be making any great plays. It isn't until the glove is filled by its owner's hand that it really comes to life.

The same is true with us. The "abundant life" Jesus keeps promising all depends on how much we let the Owner have His way—to what extent we allow Him to fill us.

JESUS WEPT

Ever since we were little tykes in Sunday School we've been taught that this is the shortest verse in the Bible. But God has more in mind with this verse than to impress us with His sentence construction. Instead, this line and those surrounding it give us an even clearer picture of Jesus' personality. Actually in this little section (verses 33, 35, and 38) we see that Jesus is "deeply moved" with grief not once, not twice, but three times!

Why? Doesn't He think He'll see Lazarus again? Doesn't He think He can pull off this raising-of-the-dead bit?

Not quite. It seems pretty obvious that Jesus knows exactly what He can do. What we see in this section is that every time Jesus is overcome with sadness it's because the people around Him are overcome with sadness.

Could it be any clearer how deeply God loves us, how strongly He feels for us? It makes no difference that He knows the final outcome will be good; if *we're* hurting, *God's* hurting.

Our Lord is not some whip-snapping ringmaster who expects us to jump through hoops every time He shouts. He's not some sadistic tyrant just waiting to push us into hell over the slightest mistake.

I'm sorry, Billy, you're just two points shy of heaven. It's the burning pit for you, Bub.

That's not our God.

Instead, He is constantly at our side, loving us and encouraging us. He is always there, feeling what we're feeling, excited over our victories, aching over our defeats.

And just as with Mary and Martha, every time we weep, He weeps.

That's commitment.

That's caring.

That's love.

ARISE!

. . . .

Read JOHN 11:38-44

Not a bad trick—raising someone from the dead. But this wasn't a one-time thing for Jesus. In His three short years of ministry He brought at least four different people back from the dead.

There was Lazarus, of course. And there was the 12-year-old girl whose parents were really broken up over her death (Luke 8:41-56). There was the time Jesus actually stopped a funeral heading for the cemetery and raised a boy out of the coffin (Luke 7:11-15). And finally, of course, there was Jesus Himself.

Four for four. Not a bad record.

But besides showing Jesus' power and proving He is who He says He is, how does all of this apply to us? I mean, raising people from the dead is a neat trick and one we may be glad to know about when our friends start pushing their 80s—but what about right now, today?

The problem with death is it comes in many forms. We don't have to be lying in some grave to experience it. We may be young and alive on the outside but inside there may be parts of us that have already died—dreams shattered, hopes destroyed, pieces of our lives that are broken and withered.

For most of us those areas may seem just as impossible to resurrect and bring back to life as raising some smelly, four-day-old corpse from the dead.

But, as we've seen, there is a way for resurrection. And it always starts and finishes with Jesus. Still, there are also a couple of requirements on our part. First, we have to . . .

84

BELIEVE

What is it Jesus tells Martha?

> Did I not tell you that if you believed, you would see the glory of God [in this situation]?
> (verse 40)

Then there are His other promises:

> If you believe, you will receive whatever you ask for in prayer.
> (Matthew 21:22)

> Everything is possible for him who believes.
> (Mark 9:23)

But belief isn't something we manipulate God with. He isn't a vending machine that we drop belief coins into and out pops the answer to our every whim. That would be only *partial* belief. Full belief involves trusting God more deeply. It involves trusting that, if we're asking for the wrong thing, God loves us enough to step in and give us what we really need.

A child who has no understanding of nutrition may want to chow down on candy bars. He may cry and kick and scream when he doesn't get his way. In fact he'll probably accuse his parents of hating him when they not only say no but make him eat his liver and onions.

But I'd question the love of any parent who'd constantly give in to candy bar demands—just as I would question God's love if He always gave me what I thought I wanted, instead of what He knew I needed.

So . . . the first step is *belief*—believing that God can and will answer each of our prayers—but also believing that He may give us something far better than what we're asking for.

But believing is only half of the solution to resurrection. The other half is to . . .

OBEY

If Martha and Mary had not obeyed and had refused to roll the boulder away, it would have been a little tough for Lazarus to come out.

Obedience isn't always easy. Let's face it, the sisters are in a tough spot. Would you want to open up somebody's grave after he'd been rotting inside for four days? Talk about B.O.! And talk about embarrassment if it didn't work out!

But they don't seem to hesitate. Once they fully understand the Lord's command, they're willing to obey even if it means looking like idiots.

I wonder . . . do we show that same type of obedience? Are we doing all that God has asked us? Or are there certain areas in our lives that we're still holding out on because we don't really trust Him or are afraid we'll look like idiots? I hope not. Because as we've seen again in this section, if we give up those areas and let Him have control of them we will be amazed at how He brings them to an even greater life.

THE END RESULT

If we are willing to *BELIEVE* and *OBEY*, the results will always be the same: the very thing we think is dead—the very thing that is rotting and impossible to save—will be given new and abundant life.

THE PLOT SICKENS
Read JOHN 11:45-57

Remember back when the Pharisees kept saying, "Show us a sign, give us some proof," and Jesus kept saying, "I'm telling you guys, a sign won't make any difference"?

To be honest, I thought that might have been a little narrow-minded of Jesus—you know, just a little judgmental. I mean, how does He know? If all they needed was one little miracle, why not help them out?

Well, they definitely have one now. Signs don't come much fancier than a man raised from the grave after being dead four days. And the Pharisees' response?

"Kill Him!"

Say what?!

That's right. But what's even more interesting is that these guys don't even doubt the miracles that are happening. In fact they are the ones saying, "Here is this man performing many miraculous signs" (verse 47).

As we've said before, proof and facts are not what prevent people from believing in Christ. With everybody, just as with the Pharisees, it comes down to *giving up control and ownership of our lives.*

Now granted, personal control can be a pretty scary thing to lose. But I'll tell you, looking at Jesus' track record with all that power, all that love, and all that authority over death, and then looking at my track record . . . well, you don't have to be a nuclear scientist to figure out who I'm going to let call the shots.

COMMON SENSE

But even with all His power, Jesus still uses some common sense. Instead of hanging out in an area where people are trying to kill Him (Lazarus lived just a short stroll from Jerusalem), Jesus and the guys opt for a little R and R in the desert.

There's a lesson here for us. Yes, we should have faith; yes, we should trust God in every situation. But He also expects us to use a little common sense.

I'm afraid the question, "Why bother studying for the chemistry test when I already prayed?" isn't exactly the type of faith God has in mind. Faith is *not* an excuse for laziness or stupidity. It *is* a way for God to be glorified and to help us reach our fullest, most maximized life.

CHAPTER EIGHT

THE CLOCK TICKS DOWN
JOHN 12–13

HOWIE STANDS FIRM UNDER PRESSURE.

THE KING HAS COME
. . . .
Read JOHN 12:1-19

After some time in the desert, Jesus and the boys
return to Lazarus' home. Mary, in her deep love and
appreciation, pours expensive perfume all over His
feet and then, to top it off, actually begins wiping
those feet with her hair!

Talk about love. Talk about devotion. Talk about
weird! I don't know about you, but if I were over
visiting some friend, and his sister suddenly came in
and started washing my feet with her hair, I'd be a
shade on the uncomfortable side. But not Jesus. He
accepts it. He doesn't ridicule her for her style; He
doesn't tell her she's out of line. Instead, He recog-
nizes that what she's doing is from her heart—and it
is the heart that God listens to.

Of course, Judas has been listening to something
else. And the jingle in the old money bag could have
been a lot louder if Mary would have just come
across with some cold, hard cash instead of spending it on foot perfume.

But as we see here, you can't buy God off. If it
came down to one or the other, He'd much rather
have our hearts than our checkbooks.

TRIUMPHAL ENTRY

The time has finally come. We've already talked a
little about the first Passover in Egypt—about the
people killing the lamb, putting its blood on their
doorposts, and how all of this really pointed to what
Jesus would be doing when He came. We'll get
more into that a little later. Jesus underlines the

symbolism by making His grand entrance at the very beginning of Passover week. An interesting coincidence? Maybe. But there's more. . . .

Way back in Old Testament times, the Angel Gabriel appeared to Daniel and told him when the people could expect the promised Messiah to show up (Daniel 9). It gets a little complicated, but according to some Bible scholars, Jesus arrived not only in the year Gabriel promised, but on the *exact day* (Hal Lindsey, *Late Great Planet Earth,* Zondervan Publishing).

And finally, to make His point even clearer, Jesus comes riding into the capital on a donkey's colt—exactly fulfilling another Old Testament prophecy about the Messiah:

> Rejoice greatly, O Daughter of Zion!
> Shout, Daughter of Jerusalem!
> See, your king comes to you,
> righteous and having salvation,
> gentle and riding on a donkey,
> on a colt, the foal of a donkey.
>
> (Zechariah 9:9)

DEATH = LIFE
. . . .
Read JOHN 12:20-36

There's a lot happening in this section. First, Jesus explains that He's going to die. In fact He makes it painfully clear that this dying business is really the whole reason for His coming in the first place.

It's interesting that all of the religions which pawn Jesus off as "a wonderful prophet with wonderful teachings from God" never have too much to say about the cross. But, as far as Jesus was concerned, that cross, that death for our sins, was His *whole* purpose for coming in the first place: "It was for this very reason I came" (verse 27).

His teachings and miracles are awesome, but they're just frosting on the cake. The main reason for Jesus' leaving the good times in heaven and slumming it down here on earth was to die on the cross.

NOW A WORD FROM OUR SPONSOR

After Jesus speaks, the crowd suddenly hears from heaven the voice of the Father praising His Son. Not your everyday occurrence, and most people are pretty impressed. But of course there's always somebody trying to give God's miracle a "natural" explanation. "Must've been thunder—yeah, yeah, that's it, it was, uh, thunder." Of course, if you ask me, hearing thunder boom out a nine-word sentence would be even more incredible than hearing God speak.

For the record, this is the third time people have heard God talk to His Son. The other times were when Jesus was baptized (Luke 3:22) and when three dead and gone Old Testament heroes appeared beside Him on a mountaintop (Luke 9:35).

DIE TO LIVE

All of this is good and interesting, but the section that probably applies the most to us today is where Jesus says:

> Unless a kernel of wheat falls to the ground and dies, it remains only a single seed. But if it dies, it produces many seeds. The man who loves his life will lose it, while the man who hates his life in this world will keep it.
>
> (John 12:24-25)

Once more Jesus is making it clear that if you want to live, you have to die—you have to give up—you have to stop trying to run your own life. You have to turn it over to God.

By "life" He's not just talking about these living, breathing carcasses we're tooling around in. He's talking about our every hope, our every dream, our loves, our hates . . . everything that we are, everything that makes us up.

A tall order?

Absolutely.

But why?

You've got me. But there's a godly principle here that *never* fails. Let me say that again. There is a law here that is just as absolute as gravity or any other law in the universe. Somehow, when I give God all that I am and let all of myself die, He takes what I've given, fixes it up, and returns it to me a hundred times better.

Now the giving is tough. There's no doubt about it. Death, no matter how you look at it, is no picnic.

But the good news is, you can't outgive God. Because when a grain of wheat falls and "dies" in the ground it eventually sprouts and bears more grain, which sprout and bear more, and so on and so forth until, before you know it, the initial "death" has led to life a thousand times greater.

When we give God our talents, our hopes, our lives—when we die to them (either emotionally or literally)—they too return in greater portion and abundance than we can possibly imagine.

Don't ask me how it happens, but it does . . . *always.*

ANOTHER TYPE OF DEATH

· ·

Read JOHN 12:37-48

Have you ever gone into a strange room at night
without a light? Even after your eyes adjust, things
aren't always as they appear. Boxes can pass for
crouching burglars, coatracks for lurking mon-
sters . . . while that vicious rat mauling your feet
may simply be the family cat.

But once you flood the room with light and see
things for what they really are, you may think twice
before kung-fuing the coatrack or stomping cute little Fluffy to death.

People are like dark rooms. God's presence acts as
a light that reveals what they're really like. Under
that light we see some heavy-duty sinners, like the
woman at the well, who really want to follow God.
Others, like some of the superreligious leaders, are
just faking it.

That spotlighting is what the Prophet Isaiah was
talking about in the Scripture Jesus quotes here, and
that spotlighting is what Jesus still does to this day.
He softens the hearts of those who are really crying
out to follow God and hardens the hearts of those
who are just lip-syncing it.

PEOPLE PLEASING

I'm a people-pleaser. My idea of heaven would be
for the whole world to come up, give me a big slap
on the back (not all at once), and tell me what a
super-great guy I am. So when I read the verse "for
they loved praise from men more than praise from
God" (verse 43), my palms get a little damp.

Now, I don't wear "Down with God" pins to please my atheist friends or hide my Bible inside the latest issue of *Playboy* so no one sees me reading it (not a great idea for Sunday mornings). But sometimes, to protect my precious little reputation, I find myself staying quiet when I know I should speak up, or going along with the crowd when I know I should pass.

Fortunately God loves me *regardless* of whether or not I cop out. And fortunately His love for me is so intense that He won't let me get away with it forever. Gradually, day by day, He's helping me be a little less concerned about what others think and more concerned about Him. Gradually He's helping me be so secure in His love that I'm caring less and less about pleasing people and more and more about loving Him.

I'll never forget what a famous evangelist once told me:

> The day people's praise carries as little weight as their ridicule—that will be the day you're really mature in Jesus.

I'm not there—not by any stretch of the imagination. But gradually, day by day, as I keep letting God work with me, I'm inching my way closer.

REAL GREATNESS
Read JOHN 13:1-17

Jesus has fewer than 24 hours left on earth. He has lots of last-minute things to say, and John doesn't miss a word. In fact nearly a third of the entire Gospel of John is spent on these last few hours—hours that, more clearly than any others in history, reveal the true personality of God.

PASSOVER SYMBOLISM

Here it is, the Passover supper—the once-a-year meal celebrating how God freed the Jews from Egypt. But Jesus turns everything around and suddenly gives the meal a completely different meaning. In fact in the other three Gospels (Matthew, Mark, and Luke) we see Him take portions of the supper, like the bread and wine, and explain how they no longer represent the people's freedom from Egypt. Instead they are now to represent *Him*—His sacrificed body and shed blood that will free us from even tougher enslavement—enslavement to sin and its punishment.

THE DEPTH OF GOD'S LOVE

Custom at this time calls for the host's servant to wash the guests' feet. But since there is no host where Jesus and His friends are eating, there is no servant. Other Gospel accounts talk about how the disciples have been arguing over which of them is the greatest—so there's a good chance most of them are pretty worried about who's going to get the bottom-of-the-barrel job of feet washing.

So what does Jesus do? He strips down to what would be His underwear and begins washing each of the disciples' feet. Picture that for a moment... God, the Creator of the entire universe, kneeling in His underwear, washing the smelly feet of men!

What a perfect picture. What a perfect example of God's heart—of the depth of His love and commitment to each of us.

HOW TO BE GREAT

And what a perfect example to demonstrate what God considers to be real greatness.

It's not the world leaders, the Wall Street wizards, the Hollywood superstars, or the Super Bowl survivors. It's not even the great spiritual leaders of our times. These aren't who God considers to be great. Instead, according to the Lord, it's often just the opposite. Instead, according to God...

> Whoever wants to become great among you must be your servant, and whoever wants to be first must be your slave—just as the Son of Man did not come to be served, but to serve.
>
> (Matthew 20:26-28)

This is real greatness. This is why the Father honors His Son so much. And this is the greatness that the Son wants us to experience.

A NEW COMMANDMENT

. . . .

Read JOHN 13:18-38

Once again we see Jesus deeply troubled. Once again we see Him having a tough time of it emotionally. One of the Twelve, a core friend who has been at His side for three years, who has experienced the miracles, who has heard the teachings, who has seen the power—one of the men whose feet Jesus has just washed—is about to turn on Him.

It's interesting . . . we don't see anger, we don't hear harsh words. All we see is Jesus aching over the loss of one of His friends.

It still happens today. Jesus isn't looking to clobber those who have walked away from Him to follow the world. But He knows that if they don't return they'll eventually be judged.

And for that reason He aches . . . and weeps . . . and waits. . . .

SOMETHING NEW

At last Jesus overcomes the pain and is able to continue. He has so much to say and so little time to say it. Again He explains that He is about to leave. But before He goes He gives His disciples a *new* commandment—a commandment to love one another. Not with the gushy, on-again-off-again, heart-flutter stuff we call love—but with a dedication and commitment so intense for our fellow brothers and sisters in Christ that, regardless of whether it makes us feel good or not, we would lay down our lives for them.

Pretty sober stuff. Especially with all the fighting

and competition between various churches and denominations these days. It's hard enough to get some of us to even work together, let alone be willing to lay down our lives for one another.

But that's what He commands. Now, that doesn't mean we have to agree with every doctrine, belief, or practice that someone else holds to. We can disagree and debate all we want. The trick is not to let diversity turn into division.

Jesus does not say that I have to agree with you on every detail of your belief. But He does say that I have to be willing to die for you so you can continue to practice those beliefs.

CHAPTER NINE

. . . .

A LAST-MINUTE REVIEW
JOHN 14–15

HOWIE MISUNDERSTANDS THE
BIBLICAL COMMAND TO BEAR FRUIT.

WORDS OF COMFORT
. . . .
Read JOHN 14:1-14

Jesus continues His last-minute briefing with the disciples.

KEEP BELIEVING

First He tells them to keep trusting. Things are going to get pretty hairy for a while, but they've got to hang on. They won't understand all that's about to happen, but He's taken them this far, so they've got to believe He won't let them down now.

Not a bad idea for us, either. Jesus has laid out a pretty hefty down payment for us—His life. And even though we may not understand the tough times when they come, the point is He's invested too much into us just to forget about us.

Q AND A

Thomas still hasn't figured it all out. Jesus says He's going some place and old Tom wants to know how to get there.

Once again the Lord explains that the only way to get where He's going is *through* Him. There is only one road to heaven, one way of reaching God. It's not through some philosophy, or by being super good, or even by being ultrareligious. There is one way and one way only—through Jesus Christ.

> I am the way and the truth and the life. *No one* comes to the Father except *through Me.*
> (verse 6, italics added)

Talk about being blunt. If it were anybody but Jesus I'd figure this guy's got some ego problem. And His answer to Philip's question about seeing the Father is even more to the point:

> Anyone who has seen Me has seen the Father.
> (verse 9)

Whew! But Jesus can't candy-coat the facts any longer. Time is running out, and they'd better get it all straight now because there'll be no second chance.

But sensing that His claims may still be a little too radical for them to handle, Jesus appeals to His past track record: "Come on, guys, if you still don't believe Me then take a look at what I've done—the miracles, the voice from heaven, the raising of the dead. What more can I do to convince you?"

GREATER THINGS

And, speaking of track records, He points out that they ain't seen nothin' yet. If they keep believing in Him, *they'll* be doing even greater works.

Well, if the fellows weren't hyperventilating before, they're definitely sucking air now. I mean, it's one thing for some miracle-worker to claim to be God. But to have him start saying I'll be doing the same miracles . . . *and greater*—I mean, come on, let's have a reality check here.

But it's true. Later, in the Book of Acts, we read about the disciples performing all sorts of miracles. And what's even more interesting, some of those miracles are still happening today.

I've just returned from a trip to some of the remotest parts of Asia—places that have barely, if ever, heard the Gospel. Here I met Christians who have been imprisoned and beaten for their faith. Here I met Christians whose lives have been threatened more times than they can count. And here I met Christians who have healed the blind and deaf, and cast out demons.

Now, I'm not here to tell you to start walking across your neighbor's swimming pool or try to evacuate the nearest hospital or cemetery. All I'm saying is that Jesus promised it then, and in some parts of the world, it's still happening now.

> I will do whatever you ask in My name, so that the Son may bring glory to the Father. You may ask Me for anything in My name, and I will do it.
> (verses 13-14)

ONE WITH GOD
Read JOHN 14:15-31

Talk about a mouthful. A whole book could be spent on the information Jesus is downloading here. Let's see if we can break into the basics.

IF YOU LOVE ME...

Three times Jesus says that if we love Him we will follow His commandments. It's important to keep the order in mind. First, we are to love Jesus. Then, as a result of that love, we obey Him. So first we establish a relationship with Him and, as a result of that love, we start doing what He asks.

And that obedience acts as a spiritual thermometer to let us know if we really love Jesus or if we're just playing church.

THE COMFORTER

Two times in this section Jesus talks about sending the Comforter, the Holy Spirit. No doubt the disciples are pretty bummed that Jesus is about to leave. But He makes it clear that He'll be sending someone in His place.

Instead of having the Son of God down here teaching and directing them from the outside of their lives, they'll have the Spirit of God to guide and direct them from the inside. The very Spirit that Jesus has, that allows Him to be one with the Father, will come and live inside them, allowing them to experience the same oneness, the same love, the same power.

Not a bad deal. But, contrary to popular Eastern teachings, this oneness with God, this presence of His Spirit comes *only* to those who have committed their lives to Jesus Christ.

UNEARTHLY PEACE

Finally, Jesus promises that the disciples will have peace. But, "not as the world gives." On the contrary, there will be storms and dark, painful times ahead for these guys. In fact most scholars believe that every one of them was either imprisoned or executed.

No, that peace will have very little to do with outward circumstances. Instead, it will come from the *inside*. And that inside peace will be so powerful that it won't make any difference what the world throws at them from the outside.

That peace is for us too. Jesus never promised to take us *around* the storms of life. In fact He promised just the opposite: "In this world you will have trouble" (John 16:33).

What He does promise is to take us *through* those storms in such a way that they can't touch us—not deep inside, not where we really live. Regardless of the outward circumstances, way down, deep in our guts, the storms of life will never destroy our peace. If we've given our lives to God, then way down, deep inside, it will be smooth sailing.

GREAT GARDENER IN THE SKY

Read JOHN 15:1-8

We recently bought a place that has a little orchard in it. For one reason or another the trees weren't in great shape—some were diseased, others were rotting, and others hadn't borne any fruit for years.

Last week a gardener friend, whose trees all look like something out of *Better Homes and Gardens*, came out to show me how to save them. I nearly had a heart attack. I wanted nice, big, healthy trees with great fruit. So what did this guy do? With saw, pruning shears, and a gleam in his eye, he seemed to be hacking off every branch in sight!

"What are you doing?" I cried. "Don't touch that branch; it's huge, it's beautiful!"

"Only if you like driftwood; it's dead."

"Yeah, but—" Off it came. And before it hit the ground he was reaching for another. "Now wait a minute," I shouted, "that one's alive."

"Yup, but it's too spindly. It's gotta go so the good branches can have the sap."

I watched helplessly as he snipped it off and reached for another.

"Hold it, Joe! That one's a perfect branch!"

"Exactly; that's why we have to prune it back—otherwise the sap will go toward making it longer instead of bearing better fruit."

Another painful snip. Finally, unable to take anymore, I shouted, "Stop! Hold it! That's enough!"

There was a long moment of silence. Then in the crisp winter sun he turned to me and asked just one question: "Bill, do you want healthy trees with good fruit, or do you want wild, scraggly trees that are going to die?"

He had me. He was the expert gardener. He knew what was best. I silently nodded my consent. And, as painful as it was, I kept my comments down to whimpers as I watched the branches fall.

God is the expert gardener. He knows exactly what we need to grow strong and healthy . . . and what we *don't* need. Even when the best areas in our lives are being trimmed or cut back, we have to trust that He knows what He's doing. The pruning will always, *always* be for our own good. No matter how painful it is, the pruning will always help us grow strong and have the greatest amount of fruit. Always.

ABIDE IN ME

Besides the pruning, there's another important part to our growth. The quality and productivity of our lives directly depends on our relationship with Jesus.

I am the vine, you are the branches.

(verse 5)

If a branch is severed, it cannot bear fruit. It can strain and strive all it wants, but if it's not connected to the tree it will bear no fruit . . . and eventually it will die.

But if it is strongly connected, the flow of life will be steady, making the branch strong and productive. In fact if it is securely connected to the tree, that branch will be as strong and as fruitful as the tree itself.

How's your connection?

FRIENDS OF GOD = ENEMIES OF THE WORLD

Read JOHN 15:9-27

Once again Jesus tells us to obey. If we obey, we can be secure in His care and protection. If we obey, our lives will no longer be sad or boring. If we obey, He promises that our joy will be complete (verse 11).

Complete joy. I guess I could live with that.

But Jesus goes on. If we obey and stay in His love, we're no longer just His servants. We become His friends.

Picture it: the Creator of the universe, the One who is receiving all that glory and power from the Father, the very Being that all of the angels and creation worship—He has chosen to call us *friends*.

WORLD HATRED

But there's another side to the coin. If we're friends with God, there's one little snag: the world will hate us. It's a sad fact, but the truth. The world hated God enough to kill Him, so why should we, His followers, expect any different?

Oh, there is one way we can get out of it. Fake it. You know, turn into secret-agent Christians, go undercover. That way we can have the best of both worlds—a little of God here, a little of the world there. Sure, being friends with the world means compromising our beliefs once in a while—you know, going along with the crowd, doing a little sin here or there—but, hey, all friendship requires a little sacrifice, right?

The Bible has a few serious words for those of us

who try to play it both ways:

> You adulterous people, don't you know that friendship with the world is hatred toward God? Anyone who chooses to be a friend of the world becomes an enemy of God.
>
> (James 4:4)

So . . . we have two choices. Pursue God's love or the world's love. The decision isn't easy. Both have lots to offer. But since it comes down to being loved by one or the other, we have to ask ourselves whose love we really want. Whose love is deeper and more committed?

Do we want to be loved by a world that basically just wants to use us? A world that, as soon as we make a false step, or fall from its grace, is going to wad us up and toss us away like a used Kleenex?

Or do we want to be loved by Someone whose dedication is so intense, so committed that He considered our lives more important than His own?

When we look at it that way, the decision isn't so tough.

CHAPTER TEN

PARTING WORDS

JOHN 16—17

MAY EVENTS CALENDAR

S	M	T	W	T	F	S
1 SUNDAY SERVICE	2 9:20 ROCK MUSIC BONFIRE	3 11AM SCUBA DIVERS FOR CHRIST	4 8AM PEW CLEANING	5 1PM BAKE SALE	6 9AM GOD'S GOLFERS	7 2PM CHOIR PICNIC
8 SUNDAY SERVICE	9 10AM USHER TRAINING SEMINAR	10 9PM DIVINE DANCE	11 2PM SINGLES CROQUET	12 7PM HOLY HOCKEY	13 3PM CAR WASH	14 6PM POT-LUCK DINNER
15	16	17	18	19	20	21

SPENDING ALL MY TIME AT CHURCH HAS REALLY HELPED IMPROVE MY WITNESS.

HOWIE... YOUR WITNESS TO WHO?

29 SUNDAY SERVICE	30	31 8PM ALTAR BOY TRY-OUTS

STU IDENTIFIES THE MISSING ELEMENT OF HOWIE'S EVANGELISM STRATEGY.

TOUGH TIMES
. . . .
Read JOHN 16:1-4

Jesus doesn't take any chances. I mean, so far the disciples haven't demonstrated a real fine grasp of who He is or what His mission is all about. So, just to be sure, He goes over it one last time.

PERSECUTION

First they need to remember that the world is going to hate them. In fact, according to Jesus, the hatred will be so intense that people will actually think they're doing God a favor by killing them off.

History will prove this out. During those first few decades of Christianity, Christians were beaten, tortured, killed, and even used as human torches.

The sad news is that in many places of the world this still hasn't changed. Recent studies indicate that over 60 percent of the world is either under some sort of religious persecution or is about to fall under that persecution. Today in some Communist and Muslim countries Christians are still undergoing torture, beatings, and even death for practicing their beliefs. Then, of course, there are the more subtle pressures. . . .

I was in the Soviet Union last year and talked to several Christians suffering for their faith. One teen's story was typical. No prisons, no torture. Instead, ever since kindergarten, she's put up with nonstop ridicule and harassment by her classmates *and her teachers*. Films would be shown claiming that Christians were ignorant idiots. She would be forced to stand in front of the room and taunted for her stupidity. And finally her teacher started to tell everyone that the girl was a CIA spy.

And that was only at school.

At home her folks were always assigned bottom-of-the-barrel jobs, given cruddy apartments, and basically treated like sixth-rate citizens.

There was only one way out—a good college education. A degree would raise both her status and that of her parents. And because she was bright, there was no telling how far she could go. Then came the heartbreaking news—she could not attend *any* university. The reason? Because she refused to deny her faith in Jesus Christ.

Yes, people are still persecuting Christians. In some places it's not as obvious as others, but it's there. They did it to God, so it shouldn't be too great a shock when they do it to us.

So the next time someone makes a "harmless little joke" about your faith or when you're left behind for being a "Holy Joe" (or Josephine), don't take it too hard. In fact you might even want to take it as a compliment—after all, they did it to God. That puts you in some pretty good company.

MORE WORK FOR
THE HOLY SPIRIT
. . . .
Read JOHN 16:5-16

Again Jesus says He's going away. And again He promises to send the Holy Spirit to help those who believe. But He goes on to explain that the Spirit also has another assignment: to convince the rest of the world of God's truth.

He'll do this in three ways:

1. Conviction of Sin. Until we know that we need forgiveness—that we are sinners—we won't ask for or accept Jesus' forgiveness for sin. Without that forgiveness we're sunk. So the Holy Spirit's first job is to convince the rest of the world how horrible sin is and how desperately they need Jesus.

2. Conviction of Righteousness. Most people think they've got it pretty well together. *Hey, I'm righteous; I don't kill or cheat or steal. I even buy Girl Scout Cookies from time to time.* But when compared with Jesus' righteousness (who's so perfect that He's sitting beside His Father in heaven) . . . well, let's just say our righteousness doesn't quite stack up.

So the Holy Spirit's second job is to convince the world that real good is not good enough. What God demands is perfection. And since Jesus is the only one who was perfect, we'd better make sure it's His righteousness the Father sees when we stand in front of His throne on judgment day. We'd better make sure it's Jesus' goodness that God will judge us by—not our own.

3. Conviction of Judgment. Everyone (including the devil) will be judged before God's throne.

And if the Holy Spirit is doing His first two jobs, convicting people of their sins and showing them how far they are from real righteousness, then people will begin to fear that judgment. It is that conviction that will force many to their knees to cry out for help. It is that conviction that will lead many to ask for salvation before it's too late.

ANYTHING . . . IN MY NAME
Read JOHN 16:17-33

The disciples are still having a tough time figuring out exactly what's going on. So Jesus *again* explains that He's leaving for a little while (His death and later His ascension) but that He'll shortly return (His resurrection and ultimately His second coming). It's going to be tough while He's gone but, like childbirth, the pain will definitely be worth the gain.

ASK

Next Jesus encourages them to ask the Father for *anything* in His name. If they do, He'll see to it that they get it—no ifs, ands, or buts. If they ask for anything in Jesus' name, it's theirs.

Not a bad deal—and one that still applies today.

But before you build an extra garage for all your Vettes and Jaguars or start writing your Academy Awards acceptance speech, keep in mind that our requests have to be *in His name.* That doesn't mean we come to God with our shopping lists, slap on an "in Jesus' name I pray" (as if it were some sort of celestial postage stamp), and mail our requests off to Him.

"In Jesus' name" means just that. We are asking for things that are representational of who Jesus is. We are asking for things that fit into His will and desires here on earth. We are not turning God into a genie who has to answer our every whim and desire because we used the magic words.

But if our hearts are right and our motivations are right, then Jesus means exactly what He says:

I tell you the truth, My Father will give you whatever you ask in My name.

(verse 23)

AMONG FRIENDS

Finally the disciples start to catch on. At last they
think they understand what Jesus is talking about.

Well, not quite. . . .

When they finally figure they're up to speed and
start pledging their undying allegiance to Him, Jesus
has a little bad news.

"You're all going to desert Me."

And, regardless of what they say, they will.

You know, the nice thing about the disciples is
that every time you or I get to thinking we're lousy
Christians—bottom-of-the-heap losers—all we have
to do is see who Jesus picked as His best friends
here on earth and suddenly we don't feel so bad.
Suddenly we realize He's used to our kind.

JESUS BARES HIS HEART

Read JOHN 17:1-19

Probably no other section of Scripture more accurately captures the heart and deepest desires of Jesus than this prayer. For the first time He lets the disciples (and us) eavesdrop on His most intimate conversation with His Father.

JESUS PRAYS FOR HIMSELF

First He asks to be glorified . . . "with the glory I had with You before the world began" (verse 5). Jesus is not on some power trip here. He knows the time has come. He knows the cross is just ahead. He knows that He is about to face more agony than any human being has ever faced in the history of the world—not just the pain of the cross, mind you, but the suffering and punishment for all the world's sins. For those few hours He'll literally be carrying the weight of the world on His shoulders.

And He knows one other thing—He knows He can back out and call it quits any time He wants.

So He's praying for the strength and courage to go through with it, to succeed. If He does, there is no more perfect demonstration of God's love for us—or of His and His Son's immense glory.

JESUS PRAYS FOR THE DISCIPLES

Next He begins praying for His friends.

First He asks for unity. It's as if He already knows the centuries of arguments and fights that are going to plague the church—everything from wars over major doctrines to hurt feelings about what color the curtains in the church bathroom should be.

Then He prays that even though the world may hate them, His followers will have the "full measure" of His joy. Again Jesus makes it clear that real joy doesn't necessarily depend on outward circumstances. Real joy comes from the depth of our relationship with God.

Finally He prays for the Father to protect the disciples from the world. *Not to take them out of the world*—but to protect them while they're in it.

There's a fine balance here. God does not want us to huddle together like a bunch of scared sheep, afraid ever to associate with the world. But at the same time He doesn't want us to get sucked into the world and be destroyed by it.

There are good people out there. People He wants saved. They're not the enemy—they're only prisoners of the enemy. But how can we help them if we hide out? What good is salt if it just stays in the saltshaker? What good is light if it never leaves the light bulb?

I think we all know Christians like this. Christians who are so busy running around with their Christian friends from Christian event to Christian event that they never do any reaching out, they never have any impact on the world.

But there's the other type too—the Christian that is so busy chasing after the world that he eventually gets caught by it.

The goal is a balance. Yes, we are to associate with the world to make it better. But if we're just using that as an excuse for worldly thrills, then it may be time for a little reevaluation.

The trick is to change the world—not let it change us.

COME TOGETHER

Read JOHN 17:20-26

Last of all, Jesus prays for the ones who will come after the disciples—*you and me.* And again He asks that we will be one, just as He and the Father are one. He doesn't ask that we all become assembly-line Christians. He doesn't want a bunch of Jesus clones, all thinking, acting, and dressing the same way. But He does ask for us to keep drawing closer and closer to the Father until we all wind up with the same kind of heart.

Remember, there's nothing wrong with diversity among Christians—diversity is good. Otherwise we'd all be the same person trying to do the same thing. Instead, as 1 Corinthians 12 explains, we're all *different parts* of the same body. You may be the right hand; I may be the left little toe. All of us have different functions and different needs.

Yet if we're committed to Christ, we all have one thing in common. We all have the same heart, the heart of God. And as we listen to that heart—as we become more and more in tune with what His Spirit teaches—we become more and more in tune with one another. It's not something we work up a sweat about; it just happens naturally. A.W. Tozer put it best:

Has it ever occurred to you that one hundred pianos all tuned to the same fork are automatically tuned to each other? They are of one accord by being tuned, not to each other, but to another standard to which each one must individually bow. So one hundred worshipers met together, each one looking away to Christ, are in heart nearer to each other than they could possibly be were they to become "unity" conscious and turn their eyes away from God to strive for closer fellowship.

(*The Pursuit of God*, Tyndale, p. 97)

CHAPTER ELEVEN

THE PAYMENT

JOHN 18–19

HOWIE HAS AN UNEXPECTED
CHANGE OF HEART.

THE WORLD'S FATE
HELD IN THE BALANCE
Read JOHN 18:1-14

Jesus is done. He's briefed the disciples on all the basics. Now it's time to head for the Garden to begin the final phase—to begin what He really came here to do in the first place.

The other three Gospels, Matthew, Mark, and Luke, talk in more detail about what happened in that garden. They describe the intense battle Jesus fought with Himself. He's about to go through the greatest torture and agony any human has ever undergone. He's about to suffer for *all* the sins of mankind. All of the penalty for our wrongdoings is about to be put on Him.

The horror of what He's facing is so overpowering that He literally throws Himself to the ground, not once, but several times, begging the Father to find some other way.

Three times He pleads for the Father to call the whole thing off. He doesn't have to go through with this. He's innocent. He didn't foul up the world with sin, we did. So why should He suffer?

And yet there's His deep love for us. . . .

It's a tremendous, agonizing battle. Three times the fate of the world hangs in the balance. Three times He nearly calls the whole thing off. The battle is so intense and excruciating that, according to Luke 22:44, tiny capillaries began to explode near the surface of His skin, causing Him to sweat not only water but blood.

And the final outcome?

His love is so great that He'll go through whatever

agony He needs to in order to save us.

Picture it—God, caring more for our lives than for His own.

THE ARREST

Judas and the gang arrive—about 600 armed men (I'd say that's probably enough). But just to make it clear that He is going under His own authority and not man's, Jesus announces His identity, and somehow the power of that statement literally knocks all 600 of them to the ground.

Interesting . . . the very men that are about to arrest and kill Jesus suddenly find themselves on their faces before Him.

Next, good old Peter tries to fight off all 600 with one sword (atta boy, Pete) but succeeds only in hacking off somebody's ear.

Jesus orders him to stop, and Luke's Gospel tells us that He actually reaches out and heals the ear. He's come to do the Father's will: to save and heal—even those who are about to kill Him.

TRUTH VS. POPULARITY
. . . .
Read JOHN 18:15-40

Jesus' prophecy to Peter—"before the rooster crows, you will deny Me three times" (John 13:38)—is fulfilled. This same Peter who was willing to take on the whole army is now back-pedaling and selling out as fast as he can.

But isn't that like us sometimes? When the whole world is watching, anyone can step forward and be the superhero. But in those quiet moments, when none of our friends will really know whether we win or lose—those are the times when it's the toughest to be a hero. Victory is seldom in the shouting and showboating. It's usually in the quiet, day-to-day persistence of doing what we know is right—whether anyone sees it or not.

BEFORE PILATE

Since Israel is occupied by the Romans, the Jews have no say over who will live or die. So they have to take Jesus to the Roman in charge—Pontius Pilate.

Now, old Pilate is a little nervous. His wife has just had a dream warning him, "Don't have anything to do with that innocent man" (Matthew 27:19). Then, to make matters worse, when he tries to grill Jesus, the Lord turns the tables on him. "Do you believe I'm King or are you just repeating what others have said?" Interesting . . . Jesus is giving even Pilate the opportunity to confess Him as Lord.

But, being the superb politician he is, Pilate side-steps the question and repeats his own: "Are You a king?"

Christ answers clearly that He is—but not in the material sense that everyone is assuming. His is a different kingdom, the spiritual kingdom.

Pilate realizes that Jesus is no political threat, so he tells the leaders there is no basis for a charge against Him.

There it is. There's the judgment. Pilate finds Jesus innocent. Yet because Pilate is more concerned about what people think than the truth, he refuses to stand up for what he believes.

But the Lord isn't done with him yet. He'll have other opportunities to get it right. And the same is true with us. There are times in our lives when most of us have sold out, where we've opted for popularity at the expense of truth. Maybe it's out and out denial of the truth like we've just seen with Peter. Or maybe it's going along with the crowd when we know it's wrong as is the case with Pilate.

Whatever the case, most of us have done it.

Truth versus popularity. It's a tough decision sometimes. But, as we'll see with Peter and even with Pilate, it is a decision that Jesus will constantly help us with. It's a decision that He will give us chance after chance to get right.

THE PAYMENT BEGINS
Read JOHN 19:1-16

First Jesus is flogged by a whip with multiple leather strips—each strip having a sharp jagged piece of stone or metal tied at its end to make sure it digs nice and deep into the flesh.

Next His captors weave a crown of thorns and jam it down hard on His head. And by thorns we're not talking your standard blackberry or rose variety. We're talking about a plant in that region whose thorns are about an inch long and as sharp as sewing needles.

Next they wrap a robe around His body, which by now looks like one big, open wound. Later, when the blood has dried to it, they'll rip it off. Remember the pain of removing a Band-Aid sticking to a sore? Picture that over your whole body.

As a final insult, they begin spitting on Him and beating Him. In fact the soldiers get to playing a little game with Him, demanding that Jesus prophesy who will hit Him next as they punch Him in the face again and again and again.

Meanwhile Pilate pleads with the religious officials, "This man is innocent. Let Him go!"

Their response: "Crucify Him!"

Again Pilate turns to Jesus for help. But Jesus will not make Pilate's decision for him. The authority to make his decision about Christ has been granted to Pilate and Pilate alone. The same is true with us. God will not make our decisions about Jesus for us. It is up to us.

The screws tighten on Pilate as the religious leaders begin to call him a traitor to his country. "If you let Him go, you're opposing Caesar!" (As if those religious leaders, who so intensely hate Rome, give a rip what Caesar thinks.)

But that's not their only hypocrisy. In a final act of betrayal to God, these great religious leaders actually cry out, "We have no king but Caesar!" Caesar is their king! Not Christ, not God.

And the sad fact of the matter is, they're right.

THE PAYMENT CONTINUES
Read JOHN 19:17-27

The cross was one of the most hideous forms of execution ever invented. And it was here, on a cross, that God made the final payment for our sins.

Iron spikes are driven completely through each of His hands and feet. He is stripped naked and raised high into the air for everyone to see and mock as He hangs for hours in the intense Middle Eastern sun.

Despite all of this, Jesus will not die from blood loss or heat prostration—that would be too easy. Instead, He will become so exhausted that no matter how hard He tries, He will not be able to hold His body up by His pierced feet. He will begin to hang from His torn hands, His weight gradually pulling His arms and shoulders from their sockets.

He'll try to keep shifting the strain back to His feet, but exhaustion will eventually overtake Him until, finally, He must hang completely by His arms. And it is at this time that His body will begin to slowly cave in on itself until He can't get enough air into His lungs.

And there, in the blistering heat, stripped of His clothing for all to see, body already swollen and bleeding from the floggings and beatings in the face, spikes driven through His hands and feet, bones popping out of His sockets, Jesus will, ever so slowly, suffocate to death.

In the history of our race no one has outdone the Romans in inventing a more excruciating way to die. But what's amazing is that hundreds of years before the Romans even existed somebody had prophesied, in exact detail, what it would be like for the Messiah.

A band of evil men has encircled Me, they have pierced My hands and My feet. I can count all My bones; people stare and gloat over Me. They divide My garments among them and cast lots for My clothing.

(Psalm 22:16-18)

A pretty accurate description. Here's another, with a stronger emphasis on the "why."

He was pierced for our transgressions, He was crushed for our iniquities; the punishment that brought us peace was upon Him, and by His wounds we are healed. We all, like sheep, have gone astray, each of us has turned to his own way; and the Lord has laid on Him the iniquity of us all.

(Isaiah 53:5-6)

THE PAYMENT IS COMPLETE
Read JOHN 19:28-42

The prophets had plenty more to say about Jesus' death. And why not? The fate of the entire world revolves around this one incident, so it shouldn't be too surprising that the old-timers kept hearing God talk about it.

- Psalm 69:21 said He would be given gall and vinegar to drink.
- Isaiah 53:12 said He would be killed among thieves.
- Psalm 34:20 said none of His bones would be broken.
- Isaiah 53:9 said He'd be buried in a rich man's tomb.

Keep in mind that all of these things were written hundreds of years before Jesus ever made the scene.

But the people around the cross saw even more than the fulfillment of prophecy during those hours. Nature itself began to writhe and complain at what we were doing to its Creator.

Sound weird? Maybe. But Matthew explains that at the height of the execution the sun was actually darkened from 12 noon until 3:00. (I know what you're thinking, but no eclipse I've heard of has ever lasted three hours!)

There was also a violent earthquake. Now we're not talking California-tremor time. This quake was so intense that it literally split rocks apart and opened up graves. And the corpses that were buried in those graves?

The tombs broke open and the bodies of many

holy people who had died were raised to life. They came out of the tombs, and after Jesus' resurrection they went into the holy city [Jerusalem] and appeared to many people.

(Matthew 27:52-53)

As a grand finale, the veil in the temple ripped open. That may not sound like much of a finale to you, but to the Jewish people of that day it was serious business. For one thing, the curtain was so thick (several inches) that no person or earthquake could have ripped it.

Second, the curtain served as a barrier to protect the people from getting too close to God. You see, back then part of His presence actually stayed in a room called the holy of holies and separated from the rest of the temple by the thick curtain. God's holiness was so intense that if any of the common people got inside that room, they'd die on the spot. Only the high priest was allowed to enter, and only once a year. Even then, he had a rope tied around his ankles so he could be pulled out if he keeled over. In short, the curtain was a form of protection . . . and separation.

But suddenly, by Jesus' death, all that is changed. Suddenly that barrier is destroyed—ripped from top to bottom. Jesus' payment on the cross suddenly makes it possible for anybody to be pure enough to stand in God's presence.

CHAPTER TWELVE

YOU CAN'T KEEP A GOOD GOD DOWN

JOHN 20–21

HOWIE'S POOR SENSE OF HISTORY LEADS TO
THE STUPIDEST RESURRECTION THEORY YET.

THE OVERWHELMING EVIDENCE

Read JOHN 20:1-9

If Jesus Christ did not rise from the dead then everything He said and did was a lie! Anybody can claim to be God—the insane asylums are filled with such fruitcakes. But to say you're God and then *prove* you're immortal—well now, that's another matter.

The Resurrection was the proof, the seal of authenticity. Without it Jesus would just be another egomaniac. For centuries people have tried to disprove the Resurrection. And for centuries people have either failed or have actually come around to receive Christ themselves.

Yeah, but maybe Jesus wasn't really dead and just rolled away the stone Himself.

Right, some guy that's been beaten, tortured, and mutilated for hours is going to lie unattended for two cold nights in a tomb and suddenly find the strength to roll away a two-ton rock, fight off all the Roman soldiers guarding it, and show up convincing everyone that He has a glorious resurrected body.

And while we're talking about His body, let's not forget the blood and water that flowed from His side when the soldier speared it on the cross. If He were alive it would have spurted red blood. But in a dead body the blood separates into massive red clots and watery serum, just as John described it (John 19:34).

Maybe the disciples moved it.

Let's see if I've got this right. . . . A group of men who have dedicated their lives to a teacher who insisted on truth and honesty are suddenly going to turn into liars and swindlers. And each of these self-seeking no-goods will be willing to face poverty, incredible hardship, torture, and even death to perpetuate that lie. Hmm. . . .

Then there are those pesky soldiers. I guess the disciples could have knocked them all out (a neat trick since Roman soldiers were the best fighting machines in the world). But even if they did, why didn't they hurry and race off with the body before the soldiers came to, instead of painstakingly unwrapping all of the burial clothes and neatly folding the facecloth before making their getaway?

OK, so the soldiers did it.

Right, the very people who have been assigned to make sure it doesn't happen, decide to make it happen. What a neat practical joke to pull on their superiors. Of course it would mean their execution for becoming traitors. But, hey, what's a little death for a laugh or two?

While we're looking at evidence, let's not forget that His resurrection was something Jesus had predicted time and time again.

Then, of course, there were all those Old Testament prophecies. . . .

Once we've looked at all the facts and carefully examined the arguments, we would need more faith to believe that Jesus did *not* rise from the grave than to believe that He did.

SPECIAL GUEST APPEARANCES

Read JOHN 20:10-31

For the next 40 days Jesus visits His disciples and friends. In fact in 1 Corinthians 15:6 we read that He appeared to over 500 people at one time.

But right now it's His closest friends that need the most comfort. Their hopes and dreams have been shattered. Everything they have lived for and believed in for the last three years has literally died . . . or so they think.

JESUS APPEARS TO MARY MAGDALENE

The first person Jesus appears to is a woman. Interesting, since at this time women are mostly considered bottom-of-the-barrel types—you know, only good for making babies (if they are boy babies)—that sort of thing. And not only is she a woman but she is a woman with a questionable past—having had seven demons (Mark 16:9) does not make you the world's most reputable person.

Once again we see Jesus going first to the low and humble.

JESUS AND THE DISCIPLES

Picture it—the disciples huddled together in fear behind locked doors. Their leader has been killed, and any minute they're expecting the officials to come barging in to arrest them. Everything's fallen apart. They can't even give their boss a decent burial because somebody has gone off and stolen the body. And now, to top it off, one of their women has had some sort of nervous breakdown—going around telling everyone she's seen Jesus.

If ever there was a time of total hopelessness, this was it. Which probably explains why Jesus chose this moment to make His appearance. And His first words? Probably what they needed more than anything else at the moment: "Peace be with you!"

THOMAS

But one of the guys missed it. And even though all of the disciples tell him the good news, he refuses to believe. "Unless I see the nail marks in His hands and put my finger where the nails were, and put my hand into His side, I will not believe it" (verse 25).

But if that's what Thomas needs, that's what Thomas gets . . . to the letter. One week later, Jesus again appears behind locked doors and tells him to touch His wounds. "Stop doubting and believe" (verse 27).

Old Tom catches the drift and finally gets around to believing. Jesus is glad enough but points out that the ones who are really going to be blessed are the ones that haven't seen and still believe. Anyone can see and believe like Thomas. But to believe without seeing (like us)—well, now we're talking major faith—and as a result we're talking major blessings.

JUST LIKE OLD TIMES

. . . .

Read JOHN 21:1-14

For me this is one of the most touching chapters in Scripture. Not only does it show the humanness of Peter and the disciples but it also captures Jesus' tenderness.

Peter and the guys are hanging out at the Sea of Tiberias (the one they used to fish from and walk on). Peter, who is still feeling pretty guilty about denying Jesus all those times, probably thinks he's good for nothing else but what he used to do, so he goes fishing.

But he can't even do that right. All night they work and what do they catch? Zip.

Then, early in the morning, one of them spots this guy way off on the beach, starting a fire.

"Catch anything, boys?" the guy shouts.

"Are you kidding?"

"Try throwing your net on the other side—bet you'll find something there."

Now these guys are bone weary, and no doubt pretty cranky. The last thing they need is for some landlubber to tell them how to fish. But there must have been something strangely familiar about this guy's voice. They give it a shot and wind up with more fish than they can haul.

John (who never refers to himself by name in this Gospel) is the first to recognize who the stranger is. And as soon as he lets Peter know, old Pete cannonballs into the water (clothes and all) leaving the rest of the guys to fight with the fish. Sure, he cares about this incredible catch—after all, he is a fisherman. But that's his buddy, his Lord, on the shore there, and everything else pales by comparison.

Can't you see Jesus chuckling as this lumbering ox splashes through the water toward Him, oblivious of his friends' shouts and complaints about being left with all the work?

Later they sit around the fire and have a hot breakfast and no doubt a few laughs. A catch of 153 "large" fish is something worth celebrating. But you know, I bet there's still a little uneasiness on Peter's part. The memory of denying Jesus all those times is still eating at him. There's probably still a good chance he can't quite look Jesus in the eye.

But that will all change.

RECONCILIATION

Read JOHN 21:15-25

Now it's just Jesus and Peter—one-on-one. "Simon," Jesus says, "do you love Me more than these?"

Ouch. Peter's mind is no doubt flashing back to his boastful claim in the Upper Room: "Hey, all these flakes may deny You, but not me, no way, uh-uh." Followed, just a few hours later by, "What, are you crazy? I don't know the guy!"

To top it off Jesus is not only questioning Peter's devotion but He's using the old name Peter had before Jesus changed it. It's as if He's forcing Peter to start from scratch.

And Jesus doesn't ask just once. He asks three times. By the third time Peter's heart is breaking. "Lord, You know everything; You know I love You." And for the third time, Jesus commands him to take care of His sheep.

Three times Peter had denied Jesus in the courtyard. And now three times Jesus has him confess his loyalty. It's a painful experience, but it's necessary to prove to the disciples *and to Peter* that he is back in the group—that he is once again assigned the task of looking out for others. It would not always be an easy job, but as long as Peter stayed humble and depended on God's power instead of his own ego, he would succeed.

John ends the Gospel by explaining that Jesus did plenty of other things but that he just doesn't have the space to write them all. "If every one of them were written down, I suppose that even the whole world would not have room for the books that would be written" (verse 25).

And Jesus' work continues . . . even today.

As we keep giving ourselves over to God, as we keep letting Him have His way in our lives, Jesus will keep on working—not only *in* us, but *through* us.

If we let Him, He will keep working *in* us, making us "mature and complete, not lacking anything" (James 1:4).

And if we let Him, He'll keep working *through* us, giving us the power and wisdom to share His life with others, so they too can come to Him and be all that He created them to be.

That's love.

That's life.

MORE GREAT BOOKS FROM SONPOWER